How To Flirt Through Social Media

Lucian Simon Ionesco

Published by Editorial Atelerix Creative Quill, 2021.

While every precaution has been taken in the preparation of this book, the publisher assumes no responsibility for errors or omissions, or for damages resulting from the use of the information contained herein.

HOW TO FLIRT THROUGH SOCIAL MEDIA

First edition. June 16, 2021.

ISBN: 979-8215938713

Written by Lucian Simon Ionesco.

Also by Lucian Simon Ionesco

The Complete Guide of Post-Traumatic Stress Disorder
How To Flirt Through Social Media
The Optimal Guide To Have A Perfect Date
How To Seduce A Girl
Dark Psychology, Nlp And Manipulation Theories
Anger Management The Complete Guide to Balancing Your Life by Controlling Your Emotions
Become The Greatest Lover: How To Become The Best In Romance, And Make Your Girl Beg You For Sex
The Blue Hour Thought to Solving Socio-Economic Challenges and Migration within Central America
Love and Dependence in Couple Relationships
Tantric Sex: A Guide with Tantric Sex Positions for an Incredible Life
Activating Your Powers
Art of Desuction
Attitudes Towards Infidelity
How to Attract Anyone, Anywhere, In Any Situation
Love and Don′t Suffer
Alpha Male Formula
Love and Heartbreak in the Brain

Watch for more at https://www.facebook.com/pages/category/Publisher/Atelerix-Creative-Quill/.

Table of Contents

To make a better world!

HOW TO FLIRT THROUGH SOCIAL MEDIA

How to be a master in the art of seduction behind a screen

INTRODUCTION

You may not be aware yet, but in 2011 with the appearance of the free WhatsApp / Telegram / Line application, instant messaging completely changed our way of seducing women, additionally with the arrival of the rest of social networks, our lives. So, seduction came with a great change, only that very few had noticed.

I put you in the background, with phones, or its more modern version, mobile phones that EVERYONE has one, and now the latest, smartphones or "smartphones" or touch phones have changed our lives in a few years.

Not too many years ago, when you went out partying to disco to flirt with girls, you met one you liked, you chatted and even hooked up, and finally, you wanted to see her again, and you asked her for the phone number to call her and meet another day on a second date.

How often have you been given a phone number you called later and have not received an answer, or worse, has the girl you met, but you find her serious and distant with you? Surely more than you would like to remember. In addition, of course, that a call costs you money, and when it comes to spending, even if it is 1 cent for someone, we are not sure if we do not even like it; I assure you that women will prefer to avoid it.

Therefore, I have decided to share with you where I will tell you everything I have learned this last year and a half.

I guarantee that after reading this book and putting into practice the techniques that I am going to explain below with many examples, your life will never be the same again.

A relationship that develops on the Internet goes through different phases until it is consolidated. First, the attraction arises, then the intrigue comes to the exclusivity phase, in which the two people talk more and more time together, then the intimacy phase in which unconditional acceptance appears, and finally arises the commitment phase.

Thus, they advise that people interested in meeting new people create a profile on a specialized online dating portal "that offers seriousness and confidentiality." Once you are inside, you should look for people with similar tastes and ambitions and "do not get carried away by the initial tickle and passion, always maintaining common sense."

Another recommendation they offer is that you do not have to rush, and it is preferable to start with a friendship, making known the data that is considered relevant. Likewise, they warn not to be carried away by the feeling of loneliness or the need to be loved and that, always, respect is shown, and the other person's state of mind is considered.

In this sense, from the Yunus portal, they consider that flirting online allows you to camouflage a bad day, or not to show yourself when you feel out of shape, but you also must consider the mood of the other person to know if they are very receptive or if, on the contrary, she does not want to talk about very intimate things. For this, the portal has the "Today seduces me" tool that allows you to know how the other person is instant. Knowing what seduces him today, how his state of mind is, and provides you with clues to facilitate and stimulate the art of seduction by playing with the spontaneity of the users.

In addition, they recommend that the person who wants to fall in love on the Internet should play with the surprise factor and use their imagination. Another tip is "change the chip because times have changed." Now, to start a relationship, "he no longer asks himself, do you want to go out with me? But you must let everything flow," according to the portal.

YOU must know the language of the internet

It is useful for people who chat in this type of network to learn the language of the Internet; some of the basic notions are do not write in capital letters, as it implies a certain degree of aggressiveness and anger, do not use many abbreviations and short phrases, since they can be creating confusion and misunderstandings and getting to the point can indicate that you are lying. Likewise, Yunus considers that the overuse of emoticons implies sentimental impoverishment.

Finally, it is important not to make high expectations when you meet someone on the network because the image you created can change and lead to disappointment.

THE PRINCIPLES OF THE GAME WITHIN SOCIAL NETWORKS

Welcome to the chat game

Over time, seduction has evolved along with technology. I still remember when I was 16 years old, and the only option I had to get in touch with the girl I liked was to call her house and ask her mother if she could get it... They were other times, and everything was much more difficult. Then the mobile phone, SMS, Messenger, Facebook, and other social networks appeared, and, finally, WhatsApp / Telegram / Line, and now today we already have many more networks that it is even impossible to mention them all.

Furthermore, if the arrival of mobile phones was a revolution in the world of dating, by now, we can assure you that the arrival of WhatsApp / Telegram / Line / Telegram / Line has not been for less.

WhatsApp / Telegram / Line is a different form of communication from the others, it requires much less investment than SMS or calls, and I am not referring precisely to money. However, I suppose you had already realized that it is much easier for a girl you met on a night out or on the street to reply to a WhatsApp / Telegram / Line message than before when the only options were SMS or calls.

Maybe you thought it was because of the money and that if the aunts did not respond to your SMS, it was because they are all clingy. Well, the reason they did not respond is that the SMS, apart from the economic investment, involved a greater emotional investment. So, for them, it was as if by replying to an SMS, they were showing you that they wanted to see you again, and many times if they were not very clear about it, they would rather not reply directly than risk you are thinking things that were not.

That does not happen with WhatsApp / Telegram / Line, because for them, it is as if they carried the "portable" Messenger in their pocket, where an answer does not mean ANYTHING, nor does it imply an investment of any kind (neither economic nor emotional). For this reason, until a couple of years ago, many seducers or seduction students preferred to say goodbye to the girl they were seducing, asking for her MSN instead of her mobile number, so they had a better chance of getting a response.

However, there are some differences between these two forms of communication; in Messenger, you chose when you were available and for whom [it was also always used on computers, not on a mobile phone that you can have it all day with you], with WhatsApp / Telegram / Line we all assume that the other person is available 24 hours a day and that if they do not respond to us immediately, it is because they do not have enough interest in doing so. In addition, with the double-check, we can know with certainty when the other person has read our message,

Be careful with this because it can give much play!

Nevertheless, despite being an excellent tool, within what is seduction, it should only be a complement to get dates, and it should be used in moderation. The excessive use of WhatsApp / Telegram / Line can be counterproductive, and you can run the risk of tiring the girl you are talking to, of being a bore, of burdening you with your options to see her again, or worst of all, with a bad I use you can get her to put you in the bag of "just friends," you know, those men with whom girls love to talk for hours and hours, but never get fucked.

Furthermore, as in everything, there are always exceptions, for example, when you meet a special girl, and when you say goodbye to her and exchange phones, she tells you that you will not be able to see each other again for a while reason. In that case, WhatsApp / Telegram / Line can help you maintain Comfort and Attraction until the day of the second appointment. However, even in this case, your use of WhatsApp / Telegram / Line should be moderate.

We are going to see all this in detail from now on. Thanks to this book, you will learn how to develop a solid WhatsApp / Telegram / Line game. For the first time, you will be able to see many examples taken directly from our mobile phones, with messages that we have verified that they work. Only by copying what we did will you already enjoy a significant increase in your appointments, but the most important thing is that you will learn the basics of the telephone game to develop your conversations and, ultimately, transform the telephone numbers you get into dates (and sex).

Ah! One more thing, to be successful in the telephone game, the initial meeting is very important, the first time or the first times you see each other in person, because of how you will carry out the previous phases of the seduction game (Attraction and Comfort) It will depend on whether the telephone game is simpler or more complicated.

THE THREE INGREDIENTS: DEFINED IN DETAIL

From now on, you should never write to a girl again on WhatsApp / Telegram / Line or SMS without using each of the three main ingredients for an attractive communication, these are:

1. Arouse emotions
2. Create connections
3. Manage logistics

When you have learned how each of them works and what they contribute to the interaction, it would be nice if you analyzed your latest WhatsApp / Telegram / Line conversations so that you can see quickly all the mistakes you have been making so far and how easy it is to do things right (when someone explains how to do them). So now we are going to see each of the three ingredients in detail.

1. Arouse emotions

Most of the time, when a man gets the phone number of a girl he likes, the first message he sends her to reconnect is full of logic and does not contain any emotion whatsoever. Here are some examples of initial messages that you should NOT ever send, and I am sure that more than one of them will be familiar to you:

Hi, how are things? ERROR

How was the day? ERROR

What are you telling yourself? ERROR

Hi Maria, I am Lucian ERROR

Hi, do you remember me? ERROR

It was great meeting you ERROR

You have seemed like a very nice girl ERROR

I had a great time with you tonight ERROR

I hope you got home safely ERROR

I loved meeting you the other day ERROR

What have you done today? ERROR

Are you going out today? ERROR

If you send this to her and you did not stand out too much on your first meeting, he will send you straight to the garbage can. Even if you made a perfect game in the first interaction in person, you could ruin everything with a bad first message. These types of conversation starters are the worst thing you can send to a girl you just met (and any girl in general) for basically two reasons.

First, you communicate with her in the same unattractive way that 99% of the typical frustrated guys who have tried flirting with her before you have, and if it did not work for them, believe me, it will NOT be with you. Different. The second reason is that you do not arouse any emotion in her, the messages are boring and do not convey anything, and if so, why continue the conversation?

I am not going to lie to you, if she liked you because of your physique, surely it would not matter what you sent her because surely you would end up having a date with her, but if you are a normal person like us, you should burn this first principle:

Principle 1: If you can get her to feel an emotion, you can capture their attention

Thus, it is if you send her a first message in which you awaken emotion in her, and you already know that in the telephone game, the simplest emotion to create would be to get whether he smiles or laughs, what you will do is capture his attention so that the conversation continues, and you can continue adding the two ingredients that you need to get a date.

To understand this well, look the next time you are with a friend, when a WhatsApp / Telegram / Line message arrives, notice that if she smiles when reading the first message, it is very likely that she will continue the conversation at that very moment, even if she is with you. Nevertheless, on the other hand, if you see that she does not smile or change the gesture, that is, that the message has not created any emotion in her, she probably puts her mobile phone in her bag without even wanting to respond (neither at that moment nor later).

Create connections

The best way to connect with her is through an inside joke, and what is an inside joke? This is a joke that only you can understand because it refers to something you talked about the day you met in person.

The fact that it is something between you creates a connection between the two, and this will make her momentarily return to the comfort state of the day you met when she gave you her phone number. She thinks that if she gave you her number, she was interested in you at that moment, so returning her to that state of comfort will make her remember what that day was like and how she felt and that she wants to see you again. This brings us to principle 2.

Principle 2: Establishing a Connection gives her a reason to think of you and feel that she cares

However, once the connection is made, do not continue creating more connections; you already have exactly what you needed to continue moving forward (with the third ingredient) and achieve the final goal, which is a date with her. If you keep creating connections, you run the risk of making a mistake, bored her, or stagnate forever in this phase and become her friend on WhatsApp / Telegram / Line (which is what happens to 99% of guys), you know, you will become that boy to whom they tell their sorrows, but with whom they will never sleep, and possibly not even want to meet in person.

Manage logistics

Remember, the WhatsApp / Telegram / Line game goal is to get a date with the girl you like, period. It is not about having an endless conversation with her and never seeing you. I repeat this several times because many men lose their way and do not realize what they are conducting in this telephone conversation.

Many others are aware of this situation, but they lengthen this phase eternally for fear that she will reject their invitation as if they only had one chance and if she said "no," all was lost (of course it is not like that, and you will see why right away).

Nevertheless, worst of all, many men unconsciously never propose a date because if she told them that YES, they would have to meet the girl they like, and that would be a great discomfort for them because they are not used (yet). It may have sounded strange to you, but it is something quite common in newbies to seduction, the fear of success, not knowing what to do, not measuring up, etc.

In general, if the WhatsApp / Telegram / Line conversation takes too long, you are screwing it up. If you want to chat because you are bored, better talk to your friends with whom you do not want anything, but if you want an intimate relationship with a woman, use the telephone game and the three ingredients of attractive communication.

Principle 3: Getting an appointment in person is your goal when using your phone; everything else is just preparation to achieve that goal

Seduction consists of three phases, but the first two are simple to accelerate the process and achieve our real goal: to get a date with her first and seduce her in the second.

If you remember, a few lines ago, I told you that if a girl rejects your first invitation, it does not mean that she is going to reject the second (or the third). At this point, it is necessary to talk about the "rejection test," but before and in case you still do not know what a test is (within the world of seduction), here is the explanation:

Women, especially the most attractive, are approached daily by dozens of men who want to flirt with them; they have so many options that they are forced to choose, and how do they do it? Putting ourselves to the test. We call these tests, and they serve to gradually eliminate and discard the unsuccessful candidates from their list of suitors and keep only the winners. Because think about it, if they can choose,

Why not go through a selection process and get the best one?

There are many types of evidence, but the one that concerns us right now is the rejection test. As far as telephone game is concerned, this test consists in that the woman with whom we are trying to meet will reject our first invitation (or several of them), and based on our behavior after said rejections, and she will ask whether we are a man who worth it or not.

For example, if you propose to a girl to meet for a drink and she tells you, "Then I cannot, I am meeting friends," one way to fail her test would be to break down and give up. If you give up, she will be satisfied because she will think that, thank God, she has not wasted time dating a guy who was not worth it. Nevertheless, this is not the only way to fail this test. If you are upset by his rejection or beg him to stay with you, you are sub-communications that you are a man in great need and are not used to interacting with women.

On the other hand, if she rejects your invitation and you do not let it affect you at all, rather the opposite, you continue to communicate with her in a normal way, she will see that you are a man used to being with women and that she does not take rejection as something personal, since your self-confidence is so high that the words of a woman will not affect you in what more minimal. It is how an attractive man with options would act, so if you are rejected, you should act this way and try again in a few days.

HOW TO SEDUCE A WOMAN ONLINE

Do you wonder how to seduce a woman? This article will try to answer your question through 10 tips based on the female perspective.

Nevertheless, first, it must be clarified that the internet reflects reality to a large extent. You will connect according to what you have recorded in your profile: data such as age, interests, hobbies, etc.

The best thing is that you do not initiate conversations with people who are different or very distant from you, this way, you will avoid disappointment when they move on to real life.

Now, listen to these ten tips, and you will see that you will achieve success in your relationships online:

1. Use the chat properly

You will meet women of different strata and levels. However, you will bond with those with whom you have similar affinities and interests, being able to establish an emotional connection. Take a detailed look at the profiles of the girls you are interested in, and do your best to create an appropriate profile for yourself. That is not grotesque or vulgar, but polite, respectful, and reflects you in the best way.

At first, think that you already have something in common with the girl: both are looking for a connection with the other. For this reason, do not rush things. Before considering how to seduce a woman online, you must establish a connection with her based on trust. Make her feel comfortable and curious to talk to you.

Do not think that you are a psychopath, or a pervert, or anything like that, since that is very common mainly in contact portals to find a partner; and On the contrary, you must increase the expectation towards you and the desire to meet you in person.

2. Honest but mysterious

Concerning how to seduce a woman on the internet, the most important thing is not to lie. Honesty is very simple and always your best option. Do not say anything that later you cannot sustain, such as postgraduate degrees or intense lives.

Honesty begins at home. Be honest with yourself, and you want a girl who accepts you for who you are, not whom you appear to be. Lies are always discovered and damage the most important thing in the relationship: trust.

Fill out your profile honestly about your appearance, tastes, personality, marital status, education, and intentions. Now, do not confuse honesty with lack of mystery. Instead, let him discover things about you in conversations.

3. Polite and respectful

This point can open doors for you to meet girls or slam them shut. For your chat date, dress up with respect and politeness. Use a respectful vocabulary according to social conventions: you talk to women, not friends at the bar.

Your level of education will be reflected in your writing. Spelling is very important, so avoid mistakes. One of the secrets of how to seduce a woman on the internet is to show you careful and detailed.

Remember: as you project yourself, they will be the type of women you attract. So, behave appropriately, and you will project the best of yourself, attracting a girl appropriate to your expectations.

4. Flirt

As conversations, progress, flirt with her with effective emotional communication so you can get her to flirt with you in response. The compliments are a show of interest but do not overdo it; make it pleasant and sufficient.

Be original by being yourself. You can tell him how much you would like to touch his hand or stroke his hair without ever verging on the vulgar; be careful with that.

Maintain a tender and, at the same time, sexual seduction, respectful always. Do not be the best friend, be gallant to the point that she initiates her flirtations and let her mark the intensity of the comments a bit. Nevertheless, on the other hand, it pleasantly surprises her from time to time, makes her feel nervous, but she enjoys it.

5. Seek to know her and to notice her

Make sure you are doing whatever it takes to get to know her properly. Read carefully when he tells you something; retain that information. Later, you will surely ask questions about what he has already told you; This way, you show interest, and the two of you will get to know each other openly.

You must be interested in her inner world, tastes, emotions, projects, dreams, fears, disappointments, in short, what has made her who she is. These things will allow you to make her want to get close to you.

6. Reciprocity in conversation

This is very simple: if she shares things with you, do the same. So, the answer to how to seduce a woman on the internet makes her feel reciprocity in communication. This will give you the confidence to share more of yourself.

Women value those moments when you decide to share who you are, what you think, or what you expect from life. In any case, remember not to overdo it. When we say reciprocal, it does not imply that you will tell her the story of your life if she has not told you anything. Do not give more or less than what you receive.

7. Things in common

Women, although they like sports and consoles, are not interested in meeting immature men. When a woman seeks a partner, that is what she is looking for, not a child. Therefore, make sure you do not see yourself like a big boy who awakens his motherly side. Trust me, and you do not want to date your mother either. Nevertheless, on the other hand, do not behave paternally either; it is just as weird or inconvenient.

To seduce a woman on the internet, you can always share your hobbies and be interested in hers. Meeting points are important. Maintain a healthy balance between fun, gallant, polite, sensual, and manly, without going overboard on either side. So, focus on the things in common. If there are not, leave her alone and find another girl, respectfully.

8. Be interesting and avoid cliches

Think about how to seduce a woman online through something you like to talk about. You can ask for her opinion on a topic you find interesting, so she talks and expresses herself.

Avoid clichéd presentations, such as: how sexy you are! We talked for a while? or something like that; girls hate that. Becoming a movie hunk does not work. Instead, ask her questions about her, about her interests, what she likes or dislikes.

9. Decent profile photos

On how to make a woman fall in love by chat, profile photos are another secret. They will not be the reflection of your soul but of your education. They can be a declaration of intent, and they can favor you and bring you down. Update your photos so that it is easy to recognize you when they meet in person.

Highlight your attributes without falling into the objectionable or unpleasant. Avoid making your photos say that you are too partying unless you want from your relationships. Your car does not matter, and neither does your gym equipment. You want to attract women, and you are not looking for friends for partying.

10. The messages

Write politely and respectfully to girls. Do not be complex or boring. Express your true self, but in a fun, original way. Try to be very specific so as not to be misunderstood.

Even if you do not know how to seduce a woman online, do not bother the girls; that will not help you. We do not want someone to bother us; that is for children. Nor do we want to be flattered to death.

Let her tell you things, and you will know where it is best to continue the conversation. Work hard in conversations and let it show. Furthermore, be original in each message: do not repeat yourself, so it will be easier for you to connect and for your words to reach a girl. Make appointments with determination, but let her bring someone to accompany her, so she knows that you are not dangerous.

HOW TO FLIRT ON INSTAGRAM?

As the philosopher José Antonio Marina comments, there is something we have all said when we were five years old: "Mom, look what I do." Today's society has many windows to exploit that very human desire for attention and social recognition.

What are Facebook and Instagram if not a big "world, look what I do"?

Okay, it also has an entertainment function and not to lose track of people whom we would have lost in oblivion in another time.

Neither goodbyes nor reunions are as intense as they were before this era, where you have not seen that friend for two years, but you know that yesterday she had sushi for dinner because she hung it on a "story."

Like it or not, Instagram is a leading ingredient in our society, and... guess what? By this means people also like each other. Something natural and that has brought us into the world: we like each other.

How to flirt on Instagram?

28

Create an attractive profile that communicates who you are.
Use the labels correctly to reach more people.
Get the person's attention with an efficient comment.
Break the ice creatively and ingeniously.
Have an emotional conversation that leads to getting to know you.
Ask for the contact to continue another platform.

In this article, we will talk to you about the most efficient way to link on Instagram. So, let us not lose another line ...

1. Instagram or Tinder? Why is Instagram convenient for you to flirt?

The answer, if you want to increase your chances of success, is Instagram AND Tinder. Now, for the sake of efficiency, it is good to list its advantages and disadvantages here:

Advantage

If you only limit yourself to flirting at night, or you only limit yourself to flirting through tinder ... you are probably losing access to more than 50% of women that might interest you.

Because on Instagram, there are many women -many of them very attractive- who have no interest in either nightclubs or dating applications.

Disadvantage

It is assumed that all girls on Tinder have, at the very least, a predisposition to meet new people. Moreover, we could also say that more than 90% will be girls who do not have a partner.

Now, Instagram is full of paired people or who will have no interest in meeting anyone. Count on it.

Advantage

As a "personal showcase," Instagram is much more complete than Tinder. If you work a little and put love into it, you have many elements to increase your attractiveness and possibilities that you do not have in dating applications.

We will talk about it.

Take care of your profile

Your profile is your cover letter. Say who you are, always biased since you are much more than photos and phrases.

Since it will be an incomplete image of you, try to make it as attractive as possible.

If your goal is to contact your friends in other countries, your profile will not be the same as if your goal is attractive.

In this article, we assume the latter, so keep the following in mind:

Quality over quantity

You better have twenty good photos than fifty mediocre ones.

When a girl visits your profile, she will most likely see how many people follow you first and then your first nine photos. So, the more you pamper that first impression, the more likely you are to succeed.

To improve in this aspect, you can be inspired by very followed male profiles, and you will see that the quality of the photographs is usually high, and even that sometimes there is care that there is a harmony between the different images.

Thematic or chromatic harmony.

32

The more followers, the more attractive you seem as I have said, it is the first data that jumps out when we see a profile.

It is sad, but the "followers" come to be the value of your Instagram, something like "how much influence do you have," "how many people are interested" ... in short, how many cool.

A high follower count sub-communicates preselection, which is attractive. "If so, many people are interested in this man; it will be for something."

On the web, you can find many tips to get followers, and in any case, if you follow the advice in this article and optimize your profile, you will also increase them.

Show your hobbies

When we decide what to put on Instagram, taking care to be attractive, we must think of three functions:

Show attractive parts of myself.

IF YOU ONLY UPLOAD self-portraits (selfies for those who are not purists of Spanish), you provide little information about yourself.

I only recommend this type of image if you are very handsome, and in any case, it can be more interesting for stories than for your wall so as not to permanently leave a selfie (self-portrait!).

It is more interesting that you contribute different aspects that communicate a stimulated life: photos where you can see good taste to dress, photos laughing, animals, flashy motorcycles, or cars, in restaurants, houses or buildings with personality, in beautiful swimming pools ...

Your Instagram is your work of art.

I magine that you go through an art gallery where there are more than a hundred works, most of them just look, but there is one that captures your interest.

Why?

It could be the originality, the colors, the composition... think of Instagram as an artistic opportunity.

Make it easy for anyone who wants to justify my interest.

Even if someone is interested in you, it is not uncommon for them to be embarrassed to show their interest.

Certain photos can serve as an excuse for someone to tell you something. For example, the image of a concert, a restaurant with personality or an interesting event, or one makes you laugh.

In the first case, it can be used to ask you "how was the concert? or "what restaurant is that? Moreover, in the case of funny images, a "hahaha" under your photo may be an opportunity to start talking.

Learn about photography

On Instagram, the visual is king. So, all the time you spend learning about photography will increase your likelihood of success.

Besides, it is an exciting hobby that will make you a more sensitive and attractive person. Also, you can get to help a girl to make her profile shine more! Furthermore, the people who help us to like ourselves more, we like them.

A basic tip that great Instagrammers tend to consider is to take many photos. When you photograph any situation, be generous and try different expressions, positions, angles ... the more photos you take, the more likely it is that you will find a brilliant one.

Do not neglect what is written

Yes, it is true that to flirt on Instagram, you must consider that the visual is hegemonic. However, that does not mean neglecting that text that allows you to put each image or video.

Putting an original, funny, exciting phrase ... or with which many people can identify will considerably increase the amount of "likes" received. Precisely when being bombarded by many photographs, the differentiator can often find a good text.

Ideally, you should cultivate writing and reading to come up with inspiring thoughts, but if the muses do not approach you for whatever reason, you can use some of the thousands of famous phrases on the internet. Nevertheless, of course, do not be crappy and quote the author.

Let us do a little test to see if we have understood. Before any image that evokes kissing or lips, what phrase will increase our probability of success?

A. "The memory of a man is in his kisses." - Vicente Aleixandre

B. "A kiss is not explained; it is practiced."

C. "With this mouth, I ate you up to the guts."

D. "You die for my kisses because I am your rich daddy." - José Echegaray.

If you have chosen C or D, you are horny, but to flirt, you go wrong.

Use the tags

One of the advantages that Instagram presents over other media such as Tinder is that you can use tags or hashtags. In this way, you may be surprised to find someone who is a fan of the same artist as you, who often visits the same joint with a personality that you like, or who practices the same hobby that you are passionate about.

Consequently, you can meet people related to you with whom you will also justify your interest better.

How to get noticed on Instagram

Instagram has a limitation: if you write directly to someone who does not follow you, your messages end up in a secondary folder that sometimes she may never open.

To increase the probability that your messages will be received, we recommend that you first do so because she knows you exist. How?

Before sending him a message, you have at least four ways to "get noticed":

The "Likes."

I recently looked at my mobile, and my screen was full of notifications. Some girl had hit "like" more than five photographs of me. So, I went to look at that girl's profile. I am less likely to do it if I only get a "like" or get it from the last photo I uploaded.

We are not talking about you going to his first photo and liking his 132 photos in less than a minute, because then you will be scared ... but you do select between five and ten that you like and give the "like." It is also interesting that they are not the most popular photos.

The comments.

Hundreds of people give the "like" button, but relatively few comments and very few comments on something elaborate that goes beyond "how beautiful!"

For example, a few days ago, a foreign girl that I follow upload a photo in which she was adorable.

My comment was, in English: "You look more adorable than a bird-eating ice cream on a bear's shoulder. A bear riding a tricycle".

This absurd and childish comment made her laugh, and she started following me, after which it was easier to have a private conversation.

The principle that we explained when we spoke in the section "do not neglect what is written" is valid here as well. A good phrase or reflection can be useful to differentiate us from the rest of the comments that are limited to putting faces with hearts in their eyes and "wows." It is also true that the effect of "that she notices that we exist" does not always have to involve very elaborate messages, since sometimes it can be simple to write an "in this photo you look great!".
The objective is for her to notice that we exist, not "that she is afraid of us because we write in each of her pictures."

Also, it would be best if you kept in mind that the comments are public, so be very careful about writing something inappropriate, which makes you uncomfortable or puts you in evidence.

For example, we do not believe that you will achieve much by writing angrily in one of his comments: I have written you a private, and you do not answer me! However, one would be more successful: "that photo reminded me of something very cool! I will pass it on to you privately".

Comments on stories

If the person does not follow us, the comments in the stories also go to the hidden folder. However, sometimes, they will read it, and it is one more opportunity to write something personalized to that girl who catches our attention.

Label it.

This is a bit riskier as it is even less unusual than the other three guidelines outlined. Nevertheless, it can be very effective if it is done correctly if the person is receptive and worth it to us to mean ourselves "publicly" by putting a tag with their Instagram in our publication.

We are talking, for example, that if we know that the other person loves horses. Then, we can go for a weekend to ride one (or take a picture with one for any circumstance", we can upload a story or image and tag that person by writing "I think you would have loved to meet Rayo" (if the horse's name is Rayo, obviously), or "when uploading this photo, I remembered your beautiful photos of horses."

The perfect private conversation to flirt

Funny, original, polite, adapted, and justified, every private message must have two or more of these characteristics:

Fun

WE ARE HERE TO BE HAPPY, and a smile is a guarantee of happiness. If a message makes you laugh or smile, your chances of success skyrocket. We will attract your attention; you will perceive us as someone intelligent - humor is a sign of intelligence - and with whom you can spend a pleasant time.

Original

THE MORE ATTRACTIVE the person who catches our attention, the more likely they are to receive many messages of many types. It will be our responsibility that our message is stimulating enough to draw your attention to the rest.

Educated

SOME PEOPLE MAY CONSIDER it an invasion to receive a message from a stranger. So, it does not hurt to "apologize for the interference" and be exquisite in the ways so that she feels that she has not received a message from another virtual Neanderthal who writes atrocities without knowing her.

Adapted

WE WILL INCREASE OUR probability of success if we take the time to see her profile, read her comments, and understand what stimulates that girl. Hence, it will not be the same how we are interested in a tattoo artist who wears part of her head shaved and uploads photos of her works, then an executive who goes everywhere wearing a suit and dedicates her free time to playing golf and enjoying herself. Time with your children. Each human being is a universe, and it is an opportunity to enjoy its beauty.

Justified

ON THE ONE HAND, IT answers the question well to "why contact on Instagram?" or "why to her precisely? which relates the two previous points. People need to feel special and at the same time understand rational reasons for their actions. On the other, justified is "I want to get to know you a little more because your photos are very original, you transmit positivity and to me particularly the happy and traveled girls catch my attention." Unjustified is "I want to marry you because you are so hot" or "I want to meet you because I love you."

You are not there to look for a cyber girlfriend

By any virtual means, we run the risk of getting caught in conversations that do not progress. As soon as it is justified or we see an opportunity, we are interested in talking on WhatsApp or proposing an appointment.

Examples:

"How many times do we have to laugh around here to be able to do it over a glass of wine or a beer?

Her: in that photo, you look like a movie boy

Him: We should go to dinner sometime and be a movie couple.

"Where do I have to put the curriculum to be the boy that Santander teaches you?" (To a foreign girl that we see in our city if our city is Santander. I must explain everything to you).

The worst mistakes according to them to flirt on Instagram

Finally, below, you can read five complaints expressed by various girls that we have asked about the worst mistakes that boys make when dating. They all have a minimum of ten thousand followers, and they know what they are talking about.

"They always ask me the same shitty questions" "They start the conversation with bland phrases like hello, how are you?"

When we see the conversations of our friends (and those of friends, too), it is devastating to see how little effort people put into making a first impression that is not bland.

Spend some time being creative to generate more original conversation starters and questions.

"It is superficial to say this ... but if you are not my type, I find it invasive."

This comment points to the issue of education that we discussed above.

We must have initiative because we desire beings, we love ourselves with our desires, and we are sure that unforgettable connections can be made thanks to our courage.

Nevertheless, to make sure that we do not disturb anyone, it is always good to take care of the forms, especially at the beginning when we do not yet know how the other person will respond to our interest.

Regarding the "nor is he not my type," ... I hope you have assumed that you do not need to like everyone, in the same way, that you do not like everyone.

"Many guys send very rude or gross messages."

"What an ass you have," "I want to give you children," "you make me horny" ... from those wonders to sending photos of penises. And that of the first message.

Please, a little class.

"That they are constantly overwhelming me, that is the worst."

We have already mentioned it in another article: nobody owes you an answer.

One of the most important and yet least named factors in seduction is patience. Remember that the human being waited more than a month to get a written answer for centuries, and nothing happened. As a result, he did not feel anxiety and made his life.

If you are offended when your message is read, but they do not reply immediately, or you check your mobile every two minutes to see if it has already done you the honor of answering you ... it is a sign that you are not sufficiently stimulated. Which, aside from being unhappy, makes you less attractive.

"When you enter his Instagram, you see that all that follows are girls that he wants to flirt with. Alternatively, to aunts that the only thing they show in their entire profile is their silicone tits ... that speaks about their interests."

This is a relevant point that we did not think about until Amanda brought it up.

When they see an attractive guy, who has taken an interest in them, some girls want to see if it is "one more" or a special interest in her alone. If he finds that you are playing statistics and connecting with all the hot girls on Instagram, he plays against you.

I hope that after these ideas that we have elaborated with so much love, you have found inspiration to link more on Instagram.

Are You Enjoying This Book So Far?

Please take a few moments to write a review of the book. Reviews help spread the word out about your experience with the book so that others can make informed decisions. They also help me grow as an author.

Please leave a review for this book.

HOW TO FLIRT ON FACEBOOK

Are you a bit shy with the girls around you from your faculty? Do they impress you with their big, slanted eyes? There is a place where you can shine and refine your weapons of seduction: social media.

Sometimes we spend our time on Facebook, sharing or commenting on the photos of our friends, so why not take this time to try to seduce a girl? Here are five ways to seduce on social media.

Sign up on Facebook

It is the number one social network, and almost everyone is on Facebook; even your mother is probably also on the network created by Mark Zuckerberg. We know it; hardly anyone who knows it can do without it. The advantage of Facebook is that you can easily make friends with any beautiful blonde you come across while browsing. You will discover much more quickly the points in common that you have with her. How to flirt on Facebook? Read the four tips for seduction that follow.

Write correctly

How do you think girls are going to judge you if you write in any way? If among friends you have the habit of using abbreviations, I can only advise you to test your spelling rigor with girls. It is a sign of respect towards the person who reads you; think about it.

Put your photo

D o you want to know the best infatuation technique? You must not go with lies. Not just because you are handsome or muscular are you entitled to it. The one who seduces the most is the one who pleases the most. Take pictures, with them you can easily please the girls. Indeed, today with an app like Instagram and the filters you can choose, any photo becomes art. Girls hate poor photos. Fortunately, with this app, the photos are good. You will look like an expert.

Share in moderation

On Facebook and social networks, you will want to share everything with your relatives, with your friends, to show them that everything about you is worth it. Nevertheless, unfortunately, everyone will not be of this opinion, and some will take you as a spammer. So, in order not to upset your friends, give them to share, from time to time, the information that you like about them. Not sure how to choose? Read the seduction tip that follows.

Play everything to emotions and courage

What is your purpose in social networks? Get the attention of the girl you want to seduce. Good, but not just in any way. No thanks to your score in Angry Birds or your benefits in Farmville; they will notice your qualities, you must make them known, as well as your hobbies. You must document yourself with the newspaper about the current situation. Post the most important articles, others, with a sexy girl that your friends will like. The most important thing to keep in mind is that you must put humor and beauty before all. There is nothing better to seduce a girl than to make her laugh.

Create a complete profile

Facebook is, first, an internet page to keep in touch with family and friends. Nevertheless, instead, more and more Internet users use popular and social networks for other purposes, such as seduction. So, before you start flirting on Facebook, you should read these tips.

The only thing that differentiates you from others in your profile. Make sure it is comprehensive. Do not be afraid to talk about your passions and what you like in life, so the girl who will consult your profile will learn more about you and know if you have points in common.

Also, make sure you write well. For example, if you write with too many abbreviations, you risk giving a bad impression of yourself.

Put some photos that flatter you. Draw a beautiful smile and an air of confidence on your face. The photo is often the first thing that Internet users who visit your page look at.

Find new people

There are several techniques for meeting new people. You can, first, enter the friend list of your friends. It is enough to scrutinize their contacts list and choose the girls who seem the most interesting to you. Then you can add him to your contact list because you have a mutual friend. For more success, ask your friend to introduce you virtually.

This technique is successful, and it will depend on several factors, such as the type of relationship between the girl and your mutual friend. Above all, do not try to win over a girl that one of your contacts is interested in. Do not turn this into a Greek tragedy.

Another way to add girls to your friend's list is to go out to bars or a party hosted by a friend. Instead of asking the girl for her phone number, ask her for her name and a Facebook account. If you want, add your friends directly with the help of your smartphone right there in front of her.

Finally, if your circle of friends is restricted or you do not like going to bars, meet up with different Facebook groups. There is something for everyone. Suppose you want, for example, a certain music group. Search the page with its people. Once you are a member of this page, check if there are girls that may interest you. You will have, for now, a point in common.

Sending a friend request

Did a girl catch your eye? Do not send a simple friend request without an accompanying message. This is too easy, and you are in danger of refusing. Instead, tell him why you want to be his friend on Facebook, what you liked about his file with your friend request. So useless, however, to write a novel, you can lull it to sleep.

To have all the possibilities on your part, avoid seducing girls who are already in a relationship.

And after that

Here you can act in various ways. If you already know the person, you can talk to them by private message. It is nice, but do not ask her out immediately; you could have air too insistent. Too much pressure is not good; on the contrary, it is preferable to take your time. Start slow and comment on some of their posts. For your part, post things that may interest him. Show that you are a positive man and that you are worth getting to know yourself. Highlight your good humor; who does not like to laugh?

After several short conversations, take some time and speak to him privately. When you see that it is a good time, ask him out, or if you are afraid that he will say no, ask for his phone number.

This might not bind the two of you. However, do not despair; Facebook has millions of members.

Leave a "rather calm" and non-aggressive comment about your status when you announce that you are single.

Maybe after five years of relationship, you have just broken up, and it is time to jump in, but not in any way.

You should not quickly express your love and tell him that you waited for this moment with impatience.

You must show your good humor and tell him to welcome the Singles Club, and you will see how much fun.

Never criticize your photos

Be patient if you see photos of her with her ex on her profile. · You should not ask her why there are photos of him since you will possibly be blocked if you do so. · You should not ask her to remove them. · You should send her funny images or topics that you like.

Make fun observations about your condition

This stage is the hardest, and it is about showing a part of your personality. It consists of making comments that show them that you are unique and that you exist. Suppose they put in their status: "I need a vacation." · You should not write: "why." Instead, you must leave a comment like: Yes, me too. I want to go anywhere.

After a few days of patience, send him a private message

It is time to act. It is about sending him an e-mail with a message like: I know five reasons that will show you that being single is a good thing.

If you seem lacking in imagination, try not to show it, this is not the time to spoil everything. This friendly little joke will reveal your charm. · Do not start by asking him to see you. · Show your good humor to appear pleasant.

Give her good reasons that will show that you are made for her, and finally invite her for a soda

You should not make advances or sexual jokes at the time of departure.

As time goes by, you will find more things in common.

TIPS TO BE A TWITTER FLIRTING EXPERT

Social networks today have become dating sites. In addition, there are currently many applications to find a partner like Badoo, Tinder, or Hater, which is an application to find a partner for what you hate the most. Today, we come to talk to you about a very interesting social network, which is very popular, and perhaps you use Twitter, it is a social network that has been providing service worldwide for a long time, but we want to ask you a question. Did you know that you can link on Twitter? Although it may not seem like it, this social network has much flirting lately.

YOU CAN DATE WITH ANYONE YOU FOLLOW

Yes, we know that you only have 140 characters to express yourself openly. However, without a doubt, they are more than enough to start a conversation with anyone who catches your attention.

Place the best photo you have on your profile

This is an important aspect that you should consider since the first thing people do when reviewing your profile is seeing your photo. Our advice is to choose the best photo from your gallery, where you look beautiful; if you have sexy images, it is advisable to place one of those.

Remember that people are guided by what they see, so if you have a poor-quality photo and your appearance is not well distinguished, they will not follow you, and you will not be able to flirt even with flies. Ok, if your case is that you are a little ugly, there is the magic of Photoshop, which will help you improve what you want from yourself. However, remember that it is better to show yourself as you are.

Follow the person who catches your eye

The good and interesting thing about Twitter is that you do not have to see the person following or hearing from them. It is very easy to follow someone and find out what they are like. Imagine being in a disco, does it cost you a lot to invite someone, right? Here you must "click" to continue, and everything will be done. We recommend that you read the person's biography, read their Tweets (last 150), see their photos or videos, know a little more about the person, and get a little advantage when writing to them.

Write to the person

Think carefully about the first comment you make to the person who catches your attention. As they say, the first impression counts a lot. So, if you have done the previous step well, you will know the person's interests, and you will be able to guide yourself to reach them in a good way.

When you have thought about how to write to the person, surely you can receive their follow back, after that you will have the war a little won. So, we recommend that you enter with something like your musical taste, a simple hello gesture, and some interest from the person; you can pay a compliment, but do not exaggerate that you do not see that you are looking like a child looking for a sweet.

Write to him

Ready, we have managed to get that person to follow us; what is the next step? Surely you will go directly to write a private message but stay calm. Keep talking to the person on the timeline, show interest by liking their tweets or photos. He will surely realize that he is aware of what he publishes, and he will see you constantly in his notifications, which will arouse his interest in knowing who you are and will review your profile.

Of course, avoid being heavy; after you have been on that plan for a while, two things may happen; the first is that the person becomes interested in you and returns the likes to your tweets (that means there is much interest) or the Another thing is that it does not prove anything. So do not feel bad that all is not lost if the second option happens to you, because it is only a matter of time before the possible love of your life takes an interest in you.

The DM is the most important point

When you already feel safe to write to that person who has stolen your heart with the naked eye (it can take 2 or 3 weeks for that to happen), it is time to talk to the private messenger. We recommend that you do not go on a flirting plan, write something about a tweet about a band or a television series that he has published.

Try to start the conversation in a friendly way without any interest in flirting (but that is what we will go to later); after talking with that person for a while, you must know what time is good to act. How can I do this? When you are ready, compliment them, make that person laugh, and, if you see that the conversation is flowing wonderfully, invite them to have a drink someday.

Meeting the person for the first time

Let us suppose that the previous step worked out great for you and you met that person to get to know them. Here you must be extremely careful since speaking through a social network is not the same as speaking in person. That said, you must make a good impression, try to be as natural as possible, and be yourself when speaking.

The worst mistake you can make is to pretend something that you are not really. Then, after you meet the person, you will know if something else will flow or not; if your case is a second date, bring roses to show interest and that you are not one of the many who wants to flirt without commitment.

HOW TO SUCCESSFULLY FLIRT ON SNAPCHAT

When it comes to finding a partner through social networks, not all of them work properly for this purpose.

For example, Facebook is not the most suitable because there has been much mistrust regarding requests from unknown people.

Meanwhile, Tinder has some users looking for a stable relationship, but the vast majority are hunting for casual encounters without commitment.

On the other hand, Instagram is not designed for flirting, and doing so involves considerable effort, although it is an ideal time investment if you want to find the love of your life for a stable relationship.

And Snapchat? A few years after the launch of this App, we can say that it is halfway between Tinder and Instagram, so it is a good tool if your romantic goals are versatile and open to everything.

Nevertheless, it was not always like this! At first, Snapchat was considered an application equivalent to sexting. In other words, it was used to send risky photos and make invitations of high sexual content, taking advantage of the fact that the images sent only lasted a few seconds on the screen.

You should consider this because if you want to bond emotionally and arrive at an eventual physical appointment, you could be disappointed in the number of people who exclusively want to see images with much skin.

Despite this, do not lose hope! Not everyone is hunting for these types of photos.

If you want to learn how to flirt on Snapchat, be sure to consider the following points:

Take a perfect selfie

Let us face it, sending someone a good selfie is like telling them that you look good to him or her.

The Snapchat camera, and its filters, are ideal resources, and you are probably already using it with a friend who has caught your attention, but you might not be doing it "as well" as you think.

Remember, investigate the lens! When you look at the screen, the result is a photo that you took, and unconsciously it projects a message of narcissism, or even worse, of total availability.

The best thing you can do is try to make it look like a friend took a picture of you, and you do that simply by changing the direction of your eyes.

Send private snaps

74

S napchat allows you to share photos publicly, but also with one or more users.

When you submit a photograph with the intention of dating, make sure that the recipient knows that you took it precisely for him, making a strategic comment.

Upload pictures that reflect that you are someone desirable

If you have just made yourself a great fettuccine for dinner, do not miss the opportunity to share it on Snapchat.

It may not be a sexy selfie, but it generates a very strong message, I know how to cook! Moreover, that is a very useful skill.

It is also advantageous that you tag your friends on a "singles night," thus indicating that you are available in a subtle but effective way.

It is all about highlighting those most interesting aspects and even a bit mysterious about your lifestyle and particular abilities.

Nevertheless, there is a rule that you should never break: do not become that person who first makes a private Snap and then adds it publicly to their story. Because nobody likes to feel special, and then understand that you shared that content with everyone.

Take advantage of Snapchat stories to flirt

Recently, at a university in the United States, a girl in the library saw a boy who caught her attention, and she secretly took a photo of him.

Then she uploaded it publicly to the college stories functionality, hoping that some other student would recognize it and help her find it again.

The answers were immediate, and shortly after, the young man was identified, thus getting both to make an appointment.

We know this is an extraordinary example, but it reflects well how a little creativity can help us find love in an efficient and fun way.

For example, you can upload some public content but have a detail that only the person you are interested in will understand, such as a local joke about a previous conversation.

Make it part of your "story," and you will make him understand that you constantly think about him.

Identify the moment to evolve the conversation

Snapchat chat is great for sharing playful messages and getting the interest of your crush, but you also must learn when a good time is to move the conversation to a more private messaging system, like WhatsApp.

Yes, we know that "strictly speaking it is the same," but giving someone our mobile for instant messaging is something that we unconsciously interpret as more "intimate."

Use creative tools

Snapchat has several creative tools, which can turn any boring photo into a masterpiece, especially if you learn to use your sense of humor.

These editing options, you find on the left side of the home screen, and allow you to add fun stickers, drawings, change your voice in the videos, as well as determine the time that your portraits will remain in view.

Take advantage of Snapchat Discover

If the conversation gets boring, but you still insist on flirting with that user, you can turn to Snapchat Discover. It allows you to do mini trivia, share stories, and fun facts.

Neither of you may be at your peak of romantic inspiration, but at least that way, you can keep the interest flowing. The basic rule with these contents is the same as for gifts or emoticons: "make sure they have to do with context."

General recommendations

In addition to the list of tips that we have just given you, there are some recommendations that you cannot ignore under any circumstances:

Do not take screenshots

The essence of Snapchat is precise that the content "disappears." If you take a screenshot to immortalize an image that the other user only wants you to have available for ten seconds, the application will notify them on the spot, and you could lose all their confidence.

Do not send explicit unsolicited photos

This applies, particularly to men. If they did not openly request a sensual photo, do not send it!

Do not try to force anyone to flirt with you

As much as you like an individual, if he does not show interest in you promptly, it is useless and pathetic that you insist on insisting through increasingly desperate snaps searching for attention. Wake up, and there is much fish in the sea!

Do not trust too much

84

As much as you trust him or her and want him to observe a certain photo if the exposure of this can cause you problems a priori, avoid taking it!

There may be a screenshot involved, and it is better to be safe than sorry.

Do not bother if someone just wants to sex

Many guys on Snapchat are just looking for a superficial and fun flirtation, and there is nothing wrong with that.

If you find that the person you are interested in is one of them, politely walk away. There is no reason to be angry!

In conclusion, flirting on Snapchat should be fun and very spontaneous. Do not over-analyze it, have a good time, and do not expose yourself unnecessarily!

IN THE FIRST PHASE, DO YOU WANT TO GO OUT WITH HER?

You got her number ... Now what?

If you do things well, for example, following the seduction method that we detail in Elite Seduction, it will be quite easy for you to get the phone number of the girls you meet in a nightclub or bar, on the street, in chat, or wherever whatever you like to flirt.

The serious problem usually comes around the time of the phone game, and if you are reading this book, it is because most of the time, when you have met a girl who seemed delighted with you and gave you her phone number, then she made it very difficult for you when you wrote to him on WhatsApp / Telegram / Line. Many girls do not respond to messages directly, others take a long time to respond and then stop, and in the end, you do not get dates with them, which is what you want.

On many occasions, they will give you their social networks, be it Instagram, Facebook, Twitter, Snapchat, or any of those that they handle, and there are even some others that are more hidden. This guide can still be applied in the same sense since you can already make video calls or send instant text messages in all of them. In a personal recommendation, I would tell you to have as much as possible and put real information, a little biography of you without getting to anything personal always to have the possible contact, and you never know whom you will run into.

When you start to become interested in the seduction community, one of the first rules you discover is the three-day rule, the one that says that when you meet a girl, and she gives you her phone number, you must wait three days to write her a message. I am going to give you my point of view.

At first, I stuck to this rule without exception, but I realized that it is bullshit little by little. For example, if you want to send a WhatsApp / Telegram / Line to an aunt you just met, send it whenever you want; I sent them the same night, the next day, two days later, three days later, even at two weeks. Moreover, what I have been able to verify is that any moment could be good within the first three days. After three days, getting an appointment may get a little more difficult, but it certainly will not be impossible. Later in this chapter, I will show you the formula that has worked best for me.

So, Bobby Rio and Rob Judge are right; the most important thing is how you communicate, not how long it takes to communicate. Nevertheless, before continuing, I wanted to make a couple of comments about the three rules they propose about attractive communication:

The first rule says that you avoid sending more than two messages without proposing a date. This rule referred to communication with SMS when the interaction required more investment by both parties. Now with WhatsApp / Telegram / Line, you can use quite a few more messages, but stick with the basic principle of this rule:

Avoid not exchanging too many messages without proposing a date.

About the third rule, the one that says do not plan too far in advance, I agree, but it does not mean that you cannot get a date by planning it a couple of days before, that is, if you have been invited to the best party of your city and you can take a companion, you do not have to wait until the day of the party to invite a girl.

First message: stick to the formula

This I guess you already knew; you should never expect her to send the first message because you might just be waiting forever. Write to her when you feel like it, and if she surprises you with a message first, well, much better, but I repeat... do not expect it. If you were the one who asked for his phone number, it is normal for you to be the one who writes him first.

Remember the ingredients of attractive communication and avoid using junk messages; with your first message, you should create emotion and, if you can, also connect.

The first thing, remember that the radar message is a message that we use precisely for that, to enter your radar, and now that we all use WhatsApp / Telegram / Line, we could also call it the mini radar conversation, since it will normally be a small exchange of messages.

Entering her radar means that she takes you into account and thinks of you; with these messages, what you are sub communicating is that if you asked for the phone number, it is because you are interested, and if you send her a good radar message (creating emotion and connection), she will return to the comfort state of the day you met her and gave you your number, for what will be born in her very positive feelings towards you.

When I meet a girl in a disco on a Saturday night, and she gives me her number, I am clear that I am not going to propose to meet her the next day (because I spend it sleeping and at night I go back to work in another disco), like this I have a mini-conversation with her on WhatsApp / Telegram / Line where I create emotion and connection, that is, I enter her radar. I make her laugh and connect with me and then tell her that I must leave her, or I stop responding and leave the conversation at the best time. In this way, her condition is perfect for a few days later to propose an appointment, what do you think?

A very good way to create emotion + connection is by using internal jokes, so knowing this, from now on, whenever you meet new women, you should prepare internal jokes that you can later use in your WhatsApp / Telegram / Line messages. In this way, what you do is to provide yourself with a path that you will have to travel sooner or later, which is the telephone game.

Here is an example of a mini radar conversation. It is about a girl I met at Teatro Kapital, the nightclub where I currently work, we had a lot more than a few simple kisses, and although I want to see her again, not being from my city it took me a little longer than usual to write to him:

> you know what? 03:13 P. M.

(Creating curiosity is one of the best ways to make sure they respond)

> What? 03:13 P. M.

> i was about to write you down, and reading our previous msgs, sounds in my head like you. 03:16 P. M.

(This is the inside joke. The day we met, we exchanged some messages on WhatsApp / Telegram / Line because a friend of hers had gotten lost, and, on the other hand, when we met, I told her that she had a very funny accent, and I joked several times about it, it was much fun)

> Hahaha!
> Do I have a peculiar voice? 03:18 P. M.

(WIN, emotion + connections created)

> Yes, more than you think, but its cute 😅   03:19 P. M. ✓✓

(I strengthen the connection ... And after this, she remains in silence for four minutes as if thoughtful, to tell me the following :)

> Well, I really wanted to send you a msg, but I was like: He might don't remember me anymore. Cause I was talking with some friends from here and we want to go for the weekend to your town and go to a nightclub. Can you go there and reserve for us? 🙈   03:23 P. M.

(As you can see, it is she who indirectly proposes the second date, it could not have gone better)

If you have gotten the phone number of a girl that you liked and did not have time to create an internal joke, I propose a pretty good case study:

> Hi Mary! after you left yesterday, a group of cougars with a thirst for young blood appeared. The things go wild. I hope that the rest of your night would not be stranger than mine 🙊   03:27 P. M. ✓✓

When to send a message and what to expect.

As I said in the previous section, you can get to get appointments by writing a day later, two, three, and even weeks, but there is a formula that works better than none, and this is to send a radar message the same day or the next day to meet you, and regain communication when you want to have an appointment with her, which should not be more than three days later.

We should not wait for a response to the radar message, but this concept refers to when the only SMS existed, now in the era of WhatsApp / Telegram / Line, we should wait for it. Even so, do not obsess; some girls do not respond, and others need to think about it longer.

I like to get several phone numbers in one night and the next day send all the radar messages at once; some answer, some do not. I take neither of the two things as something important, and when I feel like staying with one, I start the "bolt sequence" (which you will learn soon).

Nevertheless, you must not get into an endless chat above all, which now with WhatsApp / Telegram / Line is increasingly difficult to avoid. So, if you see that she intends to lengthen the conversation more than necessary, take advantage of it in your favor. You have two options, continue with the lock sequence and stay with her, or if you still do not want to or cannot stay, return her to the comfort state of the day you met her by creating connections and at the best moment of the conversation tell her that you must leave it because you are busy. This will make her miss you, make her want to see you more, and from now on, it will be easier to get a date with her.

First sad messages:

"Who are you?" - How to answer

The truth is that it does not usually happen to me because I always try that when they memorize my number on their phone, they write it down so that it is very difficult for them not to remember who I am when I write to them.

Also, now with WhatsApp / Telegram / Line, it is even more difficult not to be remembered because you already know that you can put your profile picture.

Nevertheless, if you do not have a photo of yourself (I, for example, carry the nightclub logo where I work that night), they could ask you who you are. Coincidentally, one of the few times that happened to me was not because the girl did not remember me, but because I made her doubt myself because of a joke I made, and she did not get caught. It is not exactly the situation that arises in the original chapter, but I got ahead, and I think you would like to see how I did it:

> ... after the series of unfortunate events that happened to meet us on Friday, we have a series dept with the karma... I'm certainly worried... 😶
>
> 03:31 P. M. ✓

(Arousing emotion from the first message with an example of the 99 best messages of all time)

> HAHAHAHAHAHAHAHAHA!!!
> A serious debt with the tequila 😊 🥃 03:36 P. M.

(... Moreover, it works; I catch his attention and get him to laugh; so many "hahaha" is a very good sign. The reference to Tequila is also good, we drank several shots together, and it is his way of creating a connection with me)

> Did we drunk tequila? 😱   03:37 P. M. ✓✓

(I was kidding, we drank many shots of Tequila, and it was my way of exaggerating)

> Oops~ Who are you? I think I'm confused 😅   03:38 P. M.

(FAIL, he did not get it and made her hesitate, it was a crazy party, and he possibly gave his number to several guys before he met me)

> Haha, tell me, how many guys called Lucian have you met this week? 😜   03:40 P. M. ✓

(I use the example for when a girl asks, "who are you," the "ha-ha" is very important so that you can see that your question does not bother me, and sub communicates that I am a man with options who does not collapse at the first obstacle)

> I met several 'Lucians' 😅
> Can you be more specific?   03:41 P. M.

(Makes it difficult for me)

> Sure, if it was not for me, you will still keep looking for your iPhone in the ground of the nightclub... AND! we were kissing all night long 😊   03:55 P. M. ✓✓

(That was what happened, she could not find her cellphone, and she went crazy looking for it, I took her by the hand and took her to an area where there were almost no people, there I told her not to look at the ground anymore because I am sure she was carrying the cell phone on top ... and it turns out I was right, I wore it on the neckline.

Right there, we kissed for the first time. Thanks to this message, I connected with her, making her remember all those moments we spent together.)

(Everything perfect, emotion and connection created and ready to add the last ingredient (logistics), at any time)

To close this section, an important note, with the mini radar conversations, you are already creating emotion + connection, so you will decide to continue adding the last ingredient (logistics) and making an appointment or leaving it for it another day.

"What are you like?" - How to follow

As I told you in the previous section, if you work out well when she memorizes your number on her mobile phone, it is quite difficult for her to ask you later whom you are writing to you on WhatsApp / Telegram / Line remember you.

However, being public relations, many girls get my phone number in some way and then write to me for a free pass to discos or to see what they can get out of me, the "Lucian, ¿¿¿ Can you pass us free to me don't-know-where?" with aunts that I do not know at all.

I know that this is a very specific case and that you may not feel identified, but I will tell you because when I text with these girls, you must always create emotions and of course, that arouses much curiosity in them, and sooner or later the question comes... and if with SMS the question was "How are you?", now with WhatsApp / Telegram / Line it is "Can you send me a picture?".

So, keep that in mind, when a girl does not remember you or has not seen you and is curious, and obviously, this will be if you do not have a photo of you on your profile, almost certainly the question she will ask you will be if you send her a photo. Moreover, when this happens, my recommendation is that you NEVER send them a photo of yourself. Alternatively, do it just if you think only your physique is enough to flirt with any girl (which I discard if you are reading this book).

Tell him that you do not send him a photo for whatever reason, but that, if he is curious, you can tell him that you are a person of 258kg and that you only have five teeth missing. Then, surely, she laughs, you will awaken emotion in her, and you can already make an appointment from there.

If the girl is not amused by the joke and insists that you send her a photo because if you do not, she will not want to meet you or she will stop talking to you, it is your decision to send it to her or not, but I assure you that it is better to stop talking to her (because sometimes they give in later), to send him your photo and to discard you just because physically you are not the boy of his dreams.

Think that you can use many weapons to seduce her in person, but if you send her a photo, she can only rely on your physique to decide if she likes you, so, if you are not a handsome man, this way you will have it difficult.

Date Her: The Bolt Sequence

By now, you are clear that you should never have endless conversations on WhatsApp / Telegram / Line because they will ruin your chances of meeting and having sex, and that the best formula to get a date with her is to have a mini radar conversation on the same day as you meet her or the next day, and continue the conversation with the lock sequence (which you will learn below) the day you want to go on a date with her.

The Latch Sequence: Insert Key, Turn, Push

To get a date with the girl we like, I propose three SMS sequences (three ingredients). However, since most of us already use WhatsApp / Telegram / Line, we can use some more messages; yes, remember not to be too many. The important thing is to use the three ingredients that we have been talking about since the beginning of the book in a conversation that is not too long so that the chances of getting a date with her are as high as possible. I remind you of the ingredients:

1. Arouse an emotion
2. Make a connection
3. Manage logistics

Let us see an example of the use of the bolt sequence:

> Do you know? Starbucks already put their special coffees for Christmas, and it's like drinking coffee directly from heaven!
>
> 03:58 P. M. ✓

(It was a girl I met on a night out, and I talked to her for a long time. Then, I sent my first message to awaken emotion in her, and I just needed to make her smile and get her attention...)

> Really? Hahaha! So funny 04:04 P. M.

(... Furthermore, it worked; look how different it is to start a conversation with a good message then start a conversation with a boring "hello, how are you?" Paloma was very amused by the message, and I got her full attention. I was silent for a few minutes ...")

> BTW Are you going to do a trip this holiday or you will stay in home?

(She continues with the conversation, which is good, especially since it is a very personal question, which I identify as an indicator of interest and her way of starting to create a connection between us. bridge)

> I work even on holydays, you know 😊   04:14 P. M. ✓

(Here, I continue to create a connection when I say, "you already know" and add the emoticon, what I do is make him remember the day we met, which was precisely at my work, and that is why he knows it)

> Would you like to go in a date this week?   04:15 P. M.

(At that time, I did not know if he was hinting at me, but I took it as if it were Hehe)

> Sure, let get some drinks this Wednesday,
> I know a cool place 😄   04:16 P. M. ✓

(As you can see, I am breaking the rule of writing in the morning to stay the same night, it was Monday, and I was staying for Wednesday, Thursday was a holiday.)

> Ok ok ok, where?   04:17 P. M.

(It worked, emotion + connection + logistics. I told her that we would meet in Gran Vía, and I said goodbye to her because I had to do things; I did not write to her again until the day we met.

Do you see how it works? She wanted to keep talking much more, you could tell, but what I did was leave the conversation at the best moment because remember, the goal is to get an appointment with her, not to be her friend on WhatsApp / Telegram / Line.

Maybe it seems that it is not related, but I assure you that, if I had stayed two hours talking with her on WhatsApp / Telegram / Line, very probably on Wednesday, any unforeseen event would have "arisen" for which she would not have could stay. It is serious, so the best thing you can do when you get the date is to say goodbye to her and do not speak again until you see each other in person.

Here is another case study:

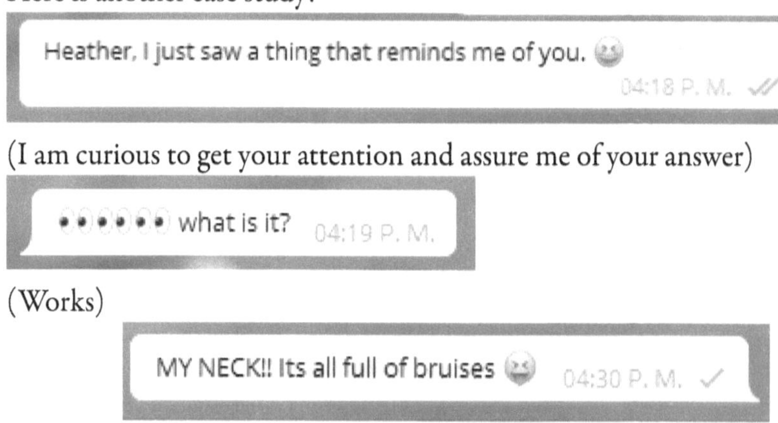

(I am curious to get your attention and assure me of your answer)

(Works)

(I met Celia at a disco, and we hooked up, the truth is that I did not realize it at the time, but she gave me a hickey on my neck that left a big purple mark, she told me before we said goodbye. I used this message to create emotion + connection; this seemed like a good idea to me, but I could have used any other internal joke)

(It works, he laughs a lot, so the message aroused his emotions, and I created a connection by making him remember when we were kissing)

> I did not tell you, but I had an important meeting, and there we were, with the heating on full blast and I with the scarf on ... 😅
>
> 04:37 P. M.

(All this happened for real, and I told him about it to continue strengthening the connection)

> Ow! Really?! Poor of you...   04:40 P. M.

(It seems to work)

> Yeah, you're going to have to make it up to me 😄   04:42 P. M.

(Here I get playful, but always with the sole objective of getting a date with her)

> 😄 with what?   04:43 P. M.

(I play along)

> Hmm.. what comes to your mind? 😆   04:44 P. M.

(I am still playing)

> All you want is a rain of kisses 😘 😘 😘   04:45 P. M.

(It is another inside joke. The day we met, she asked me to tell her something personal, and I told her that I would tell her, but in exchange for something. She replied that if I told her, in exchange, she would give me " kisses," the truth is that his answer made me laugh a lot; Celia is an 18-year-old girl more than adorable.

If you notice, this message is excellent because she is the one who is using an internal joke to create emotion + connection with me; I am ready to pull the trigger and use the logistics)

(I put the logistics in the game, and I invite her to see us at a party called FUNK KOMBAT so that she can compensate me for my purple neck)

(The bolt sequence worked perfectly)

Are You Enjoying This Book So Far?

Please take a few moments to write a review of the book. Reviews help spread the word out about your experience with the book so that others can make informed decisions. They also help me grow as an author.

Please leave a review for this book.

If She is Difficult: Dating Girls Who Do not Respond

What if she does not answer

It is necessary to remind you that for the phone game to work normally and get an appointment with her, it is very important to have done things right when you met and exchanged phone numbers. Because if you did not do it well, it is possible that she gave you her number just for education or simply because she was in a hurry to tell you no, and if this is what happened, it does not matter that later you are the best in the world in the WhatsApp game / Telegram / Line because you literally would not stand a chance. It is important to do things right from the beginning.

She Has Little Interest: How to Get Her Excited for a Date

The game ends only when the girl we are trying to meet sends us an SMS asking or demanding that we stop writing to her. Now in the era of WhatsApp / Telegram / Line, this will no longer be necessary because if a girl does not want to know anything about you, what she will do is block you. It may sound a bit cruel, but if you think about it, it is the best for everyone, she will get rid of you easily, and you will stop wasting time.

How to know if a girl has blocked you? Normally if 48 hours pass and you do not see in the image of your WhatsApp / Telegram / Line the double-check that accompanies the messages that have been read, it is because she has blocked you. NO girl in the world spends more than 48 hours without consulting her WhatsApp / Telegram / Line, so if she has not read your messages, there is no doubt you are blocked.

Now, if she has not blocked you (or asked you to stop writing to her), the game continues, even if she does not respond to your messages. I have realized that the best option is to try once a week or every two weeks. This is a way to be persistent without being heavy. Furthermore, very importantly, never forget to remain playful; it is the only way to get something with a girl who does not respond.

Here is a very good trick, and that is that if you send a message a week to a girl and you verify that she, even if she does not respond, continues reading and does not block you, it is most likely that she will end up responding (and you can use the bolt sequence). So, if I did not want to know anything about you, I would block you; this is so.

She has something of interest: Get more than one connection

This section is very interesting because I have lived it several times and surely you have also experienced similar situations if you have known seduction for a long time. There are times when you meet a girl in a nightclub, you have a great time together, you hook up, and then she never responds to your messages, and you keep thinking,

What did the hell happen?

Well, what has surely happened is that that girl usually does not end up kissing with guys on their party nights; she did it with you because you seduced her, and then the next day, she got what we call the buyer's remorse in seduction.

You know, we usually call buyer's remorse when a person buys something in a way impulsive or an emotional state of caprice, only to regret your purchase later. Seduction is when she can get carried away by her attraction or sexual arousal towards you, only to regret it later.

It is one of the "bad" things that being good at flirting with women entails, and it is that sometimes you will be able to create an attraction in them so quickly that they will end up kissing you (or sleeping with you) before you have created comfort and trust. Solid enough that that relationship could extend into something more than that first night. The next day the girls feel easy and think that you are a flirt who does that every night and with everyone, and many times they do not want to see you again for this reason.

So that you can see it more clearly, I am going to tell you in detail what happened with Jessica so that you take it into account, and it does not happen to you when you find a girl that you like:

The day I met Jessica was quite special; I had had a problem at work, and then she appeared, from the outset, I thought she was very pretty, but after talking for a while, I loved it. I can say that I made a perfect game with her; I followed the Seduction Method step by step in our book Elite Seduction and something like in an hour, we were already kissing. The final part was like this:

Jessica: Look, in this one, I go out with my friends (she shows me a photo on her mobile)

Lucian: Very pretty.

Jessica: Thank you.

Lucian: You are welcome ... But I said that your friends are beautiful, not that you are ... (I said this with a very playful tone, so I did not know if I was half-serious and half-joking or what)

Jessica: jjjmmmm, do I not look pretty to you? (She gets a little angry because, even though she knows she is gorgeous, she cannot quite see if I am joking)

Lucian: Do you want to know if you look pretty to me?

Jessica: Yes ... (and here I kissed her, it was my way of showing her how pretty she looked to me and that the previous thing had just been a joke)

Nevertheless, something went wrong, suddenly she realized what she was doing and stopped in her tracks, she told me that she had never hooked up in a disco with a guy she had just met and that I sure did that every night. So, I told her that I did it about 5 or 6 times a night; I told her to exaggerate and take away the issue, but she took it seriously, and it was even worse.

I liked Jessica, so I stopped joking and told her that I wanted to see her again, she stayed all night talking to me, but she only kissed me again when we said goodbye. So, after a while, I sent him the following message to create a connection and let him know that everything we talked about was serious.

> Do you remember how I save your contact on my phone? 😊

(It is an inside joke. When she gave me her number, I asked her how she wanted me to write it down, and she told me "Pon Jessica Guapa" to continue with the story I just told you about when we had kissed; she liked it a lot. My goal was to awaken emotion and create a connection so that she knew that I wanted to see her again. Do you sign up for this trick because it is very good? Whenever you memorize her number, ask her how she wants you to write it down, it will be normal that you can get an inside joke for the phone game, and then if you send the message "Do you remember how I memorized you?" you can easily arouse emotion and create a connection)

(It worked, emotion + connection, we said goodbye and said good night, and I went to bed wishing that the following week would come to see her again)

It seemed that everything was perfect, but it was not; Jessica felt the buyer's remorse the next day. Six days later, I wrote to him, and he did not reply, four days later the same, thirteen days later the same, five days later, my messages were still unanswered.

Usually, I never insist that much, but Jessica was a girl worth insisting on, at least if she kept reading my messages and did not block me or ask me to stop writing to her.

Until in the end, something like a month later, he ended up answering me. He sent me a very long message in which she told me that he was very happy to have spent that night with me and that it was worth it; he apologized for not having answered me in all this time and explained that it was due to some personal problems. She ended up telling me that she was back with her ex-boyfriend and telling me that she was very sorry.

I do not know if it is true that she returned with her ex-boyfriend if she was already going out with him the day we hooked up, or it was an excuse she made up; the question is that if everything went wrong, it is because I was too fast with her the night we met. So, keep that in mind for when you meet a girl that you like, maybe you should slow down, get her phone, and get a second date with her. This way, you can make things come up in a more "normal" way for her, and she will not think you are a flirt.

Overcoming the passage of time: How to revive an old number

Above all, it will happen to you when you go out a lot and get many numbers, you will keep them in your phone book, and there will always be numbers that you will not use because you will like some girls more than others or simply because you will prefer to use the new numbers rather than keep trying with the old ones.

Nevertheless, it could also happen that you met a girl that you liked a lot and that you stopped writing to her for some reason. That happened to Sara, a girl from Seville that I met at a party at the Autonomous University. Between week he lived too far away to stay, and the three weekends in a row that I wrote to him he was going to his town to be with his family, so I stopped sending him messages for a while. Then, a few months later, revive your number. Here the example:

(Again, creating curiosity from the first message to capture their attention and ensure their response)

(Works)

> About that and how tragic it would be that we would never see each other again ...
>
> 06:31 P. M. ✓

(That was exactly how it happened, she came and entered me that way, we were joking for a long time about her little shame, so I thought it would be a good idea to go back to that moment to awaken emotion and create a connection between us. I use the template message to revive old numbers.)

> HAHAHAHAHAHAHAHAHAHAHAHAHAHAHA   06:31 P. M.

(As long as they answer like this, things are going well; he told me that he did not go to Seville so much on weekends because he had made many friends in the city and preferred to stay. From this message, I normally continued with the bolt sequence until we returned. to see us)

Girls You Cannot Date: The Waiting Time

We have already repeated several times that the sole objective of the phone game or WhatsApp / Telegram / Line is to get appointments, no more. However, there are always exceptions, for example, when you meet a special girl, and when you say goodbye to her and exchange phones, she tells you that you will not be able to see each other again for a while because of being. In that case, WhatsApp / Telegram / Line can help you maintain comfort and attraction until the day of the second appointment.

This is what happened to me with Laura, an architecture student I met just on her last holiday before her "cloistered" exam time. I used WhatsApp / Telegram / Line with her to maintain interest, attraction, and comfort, and it is funny because when I did, I still did not know, but I used two of the three ingredients of the lock sequence: arousing emotions and create connections.

The only thing I failed to do was let her make the conversations too long; exchanging a few messages would have been enough to stir emotions and create connections and ultimately stay on her radar (and on her mind).

I put here part of the conversation so you can see how I carried it:

> Hahaha; Are you coming all the way long?  06:42 P. M. ✓

> Do you doubt it? I serve you as an image and interpret. I speak three languages, and I smile and dance ... hahaha and I speak a lot, what more do you want? 06:45 P. M.

> What else could I ask for is the complete package, more than fine, and I'll wait for you then on the bus tonight 06:47 P. M. ✓

This for example. That day a conversation arose about Ibiza, I told her that I would go in August with some friends for work and have fun, and she began to convince me to take her with me.

She was not serious, no one goes on a trip with someone she has just met at a disco, but the fact of proposing it, of talking about where we would go and what we would do together, is her way of expressing that for her it enters There is a connection and not now, but in the future, we could do something similar. So, as you can see, talking about travel is a great way to connect and stay on their radar.

On the other hand, I must admit that in the end, I ended up fucking it with Laura, and that happened to me because I talked too much; one day, I hinted that I had hooked up with another girl, and she stopped talking to me. I have already learned from my mistake; from now on, the WhatsApp / Telegram / Line is only to get appointments or to stay on the radar of the girls who cannot meet in a certain period, never for endless conversations where a step in a fake can leave you out.

Bad Behavior Files: When Good Girls Be Bad

S hred their negative responses

It is true, there are times when good girls misbehave, even if it seems like there is no reason for it, and you keep thinking ... "But why does he behave like this?" This is the case of Isabell, a Norwegian girl I have been dating for a while, but for no reason, we stopped seeing each other.

Last month we met again, we hooked up again, and we talked about how good we were together and how little sense it made not to see each other. It so happened that we were both going to Valencia that week because of the fails, so he told me to meet there to show him the city.

During all the failures, he passed from my WhatsApp / Telegram / Line messages, we returned to my hometown, and he kept passing me, he replied, but to put me off, he told me that his friend was ill, that she was far away, that he had not read my messages ... Until I wrote the following:

"I love girls who play tough, and here you are, acting like one of them."

(Which comes to say, "ha-ha, sorry, I am tired, and I am going to sleep now. Let us talk soon, a kiss")

Moreover, there the conversation ended, I honestly thought that the thing had not ended very well, I, of course, I was not going to write more ... Nevertheless, a few days later it was she who wrote to me to stay.

An accurate and wide shot of pop culture

Women love pop culture, make no mistake about that, and assure you that it is a powerful way to awaken emotions and create connections with it (and therefore also get on a date). So, if the subject comes up, it will not hurt to find out about the favorite series, books, or movies of the girl you want to hook up with because later, you can use them to your advantage in WhatsApp / Telegram / Line game.

You can take a chance and make references to pop culture without being sure that she will get the joke, but I do not advise it, and if you do, it is best if they are wide shots (comments on things that anyone her age Should know). If you make a joke concerning pop culture and she does not get it, it will be difficult for you to redirect the interaction on the right track. I prefer to make accurate shooting references, but I always try to find out beforehand what their tastes are (and the more geeks, the better) and then use them to my advantage.

Here is a case study on how to go from a shotgun pop culture reference to a quote:

> I have seen the first two chapters of misfits, and apart from being very geeky, I have a question.

(Paula had been at my house and called me a geek when she saw the Lord of the Rings movies on the shelf in my room. I told her that she was surely a bit of a geek, and I asked her to tell me which series and he liked movies... there we started a very funny "discussion" about who of the two was freakier.

One of the series that he likes is Misfits, and it is about a group of British teenagers serving time doing community service. Suddenly one day, in the middle of a strange storm, lightning strikes them, granting them different powers (as if they were superheroes).

As always, with this first message, I try to create an emotion and get their attention.)

> Hahaha, shut your question

(Works)

> If one day we are walking and suddenly we are struck by lightning, what would our powers be?

(Reference to pop culture, it is my way of creating a connection between the two)

> Well, I don't know. But looks you're more geek than me. You just showed me that

(It works, it does not continue with the Misfits theme, but it goes back to the discussion we had at my house about who of them were both more geeks. It is his way of creating a connection between the two)

> Ha-ha you are as Geek as me!

(I continue to strengthen the connection)

> Hahahaha true, but you need to recognize that you are more geek than me
>
> 04:26 P. M.

(And she does too, now is the best time to pull the trigger and handle the logistics)

> hmm.. i have my doubts... How about if we discuss this later while we drink something?
>
> 04:27 P. M. ✓

(I add the third ingredient and propose the appointment)

> Ok   04:27 P. M.

(Works)

> How about at 20:30 at #$%& bar?   04:27 P. M. ✓✓

> Fine, Lucy   04:28 P. M.

Overcoming Excuses: Changing Your Mind

Many women make excuses, and we could say that it is as if it was a way of doing sports. For this reason, the best thing you can do when a girl you had been with sends you a message by WhatsApp canceling the appointment is not to bother, that it does not affect you at all, and continue talking to her as if things were following their normal course. If you keep being persistent and funny, the date will come.

And why all those excuses? They can give them for various reasons. It could be that the girl had an unforeseen event ... but honestly, this will be the least likely. The normal thing is that if she gives you an excuse, she was doubtful about meeting you; she said yes and then thought better of it. These doubts can come out of nowhere since women are very doubtful, or they can also appear because you did something wrong.

Furthermore, if you did something wrong, you must already imagine what it is. Remember that you should never have endless WhatsApp / Telegram / Line conversations with the girls you want to flirt with because the longer you talk to her, the more chances you will have to screw her up. Alternatively, maybe you do not screw it up, and the only thing you get is just that it gets tired or bored of you. So, once you have got your date, drop the conversation, period.

There is another possibility, and maybe those excuses are just a test, you know, women love to test us. She will cancel your appointment to see how you react; if she sees that you are upset or that you are very disappointed, she will see that you are a guy of little value, not used to meeting girls, that you got it with her, and that when she sees that the data is escaped from your hands, you collapse like any loser. Nevertheless, on the other hand, if you are upset or disappointed, she will stay home thinking, "Buff, thank goodness that in the end, I did not meet this guy..."

However, if you react in a normal, persistent, and funny way, he will see that you are a very confident guy, used to being with girls and that for that reason, he does not fall apart or be disappointed when one makes rudeness to him. If she notices that she has not bothered you and you continue to be persistent and playful, you have passed the test, and the appointment with her will come sooner or later.

I repeat it, so you do not forget, always persistent and fun and playful.

> Hahahaha, I'm pretty sick, full of snot, I don't feel well   04:30 P. M.

(Do the excuses start, this time it was a test, note that I was not canceling the appointment yet, but I was preparing for it, what Carla expected of me is that I respond in the way that a typically frustrated uncle would, with something like "So we do not see each other today?)

> Hehe, the truth is that it does not sound very good, but do you know what the best medicine for those snots is? The gin and tonics in a ball glass with the attractive guys named Lucian. 😎

(With this message, I am persistent and playful)

> I'm pretty fucked up 😅 😅 I need pampering 😹 😹

(It seems to work)

> Ok, then how about if we meet together at midday?

(I pull the trigger and handle the logistics again to get the appointment, that is, I remain persistent)

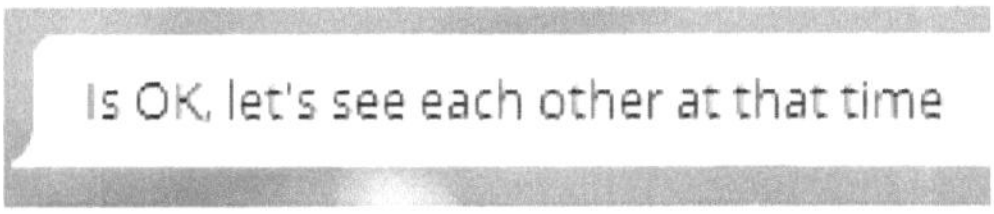

Is OK, let's see each other at that time

(Test passed and mini point for me)

When to Call: The Final Resource

We are still in the first phase, that is, when you have not yet had your first date alone. In this phase, I would recommend avoiding the call as much as possible, explaining why. First, because girls love WhatsApp / Telegram / Line, so if you have sent her several messages and she has not responded, it is possibly because she does not want to know anything about you, so if you call her, she will not take it and if she does, her answer will not be very pleasant.

The second reason is that we are all very busy these days, and if you call her and catch her at the wrong time, your chances of getting a date with her will fall apart. Because that is how it is, every time you call her, and she does not take it, and it does not matter if it is because she cannot, your options get a date decrease. Calling her would be an unnecessary way to risk yourself.

Furthermore, even if you catch it at a good time, it is much easier for you to screw it up and spoil everything in a call than talking on WhatsApp / Telegram / Line.

So, in short, the only case in which I would recommend calling is when a girl gives you an excuse not to go on a date. If you call her right away to be persistent and playful, you could save the situation.

PART 3: The second phase ... You are almost dating her

The first date and beyond

If you already had a date alone with her and it went well, from now on everything will be much easier, but that does not mean that you must relax completely. On the contrary, you must keep doing things right because any mistake can be fatal with women.

The differences with the first phase regarding the use of WhatsApp / Telegram / Line are clear, now you will be able to have somewhat longer conversations, and you will not have the "obligation" to have to end them in an appointment proposal that happened in the first phase. But be careful, do not get too long (no matter how much she insists), it is advisable not to spend more than

10 minutes exchanging messages.

Arriving for the appointment: Prepare for Success

I still think that the ideal way to start an appointment is to be 10 minutes late. If you are punctual, what you are sub communicating is that you are a good boy, and I suppose by now you know that women do not like good boys.

If you are a few minutes late, you will find your girl a little anxious, looking everywhere, looking for where you appear (and worried about whether you will appear), causing her great relief the moment she finds you. What you do with this tactic is to start the date with energy that benefits you.

I agree with Bobby and Rob that you should use WhatsApp / Telegram / Line to warm up before arriving for your appointment, sending a message that awakens their emotions and achieves a lot when you meet easier to break the ice.

My examples are excellent, and I have used them with great success (especially the first one), but they are all for when you arrive before her.

If you want an example of a message for when you are late, and she is waiting for you, the following I learned may help you:

> I'm fighting with some dragons, and it will take me about ten minutes to get to your princess castle ...   04:38 P. M. ✓

Getting the second date: Keeping her interested and engaged

The days after: How to keep the fire going

After your first date alone, and especially if you were successful in it (which I do not doubt about if you have read our previous book Elite Seduction), you should resume the interaction on WhatsApp / Telegram / Line the next day.

At that moment is when you can go a little longer in the exchange of messages without having to end the conversation by proposing a date, you will do that a few days later, when you want to meet her.

You must keep in mind that you must awaken emotions and create connections; any message that does not achieve one of these two purposes does not send it. Here is a case study:

> I will send a picture to you, can you see it?

(I pretend I am asking her if her cell phone can receive photos, which I take for granted if she has WhatsApp / Telegram / Line. What I am doing with this message is creating curiosity and getting her attention, she knows we did photos on the date we had the night before, and you also know that I mean one of them)

> Yes, of course, send it to me

(Response very quickly)

> I warn you that they are the most beautiful boy and girl at last night's party ...
> and well in the whole country too   04:40 P. M. ✓

(I get playful, and I get her to be even more curious, I create a connection between the two by reminding her of what we did the night before and the compliment in an attractive way with a couple of compliments, the latter we will see later)

Hahaha, ok, send it

(It works! At this moment, I stay in silence for a few minutes without saying anything and, of course, without sending the photo to him)

Please, I'm curious

(I manage to capture his attention fully, surely, he did not take his eyes off the screen of his mobile)

(I send you a photo in which we both appeared)

Yeah, we are gorgeous

(She keeps strengthening the connection between the two and attractively flatters me)

Yes! together we are always going to be awesome!

(I also follow the game and reinforce the connection)

Of course, what about my jacket?

(Although it may not seem like it, this message is very good. She slept at my house and forgot her jacket, but she is not asking me why she is worried about losing it; it is her way of suggesting that we meet again. So, from now on already.

You know, if you see that a girl leaves your house the next morning and forgets something, give it to her quickly if you do not want to see her again, if everything went well, maybe you should forget the earrings on your bedside table.

> Your jackter its pretty great in here, it just asked about you 😊
>
> 04:43 P. M. ✓

(I play the game, excitement + connection)

> Haha! Well well, then one day I will go for it and let's have dinner together
>
> 04:43 P. M.

(Note that I wrote to Lara the next day with the sole purpose of "keeping the fire" between us, and in the end, in a small exchange of messages, it was she who proposed new date. Most of the time, things will work out for you. fine, but many of them will turn out even better than you expected)

Schedule the second appointment

Getting a second date alone with her should not be very complicated, so act normally; you know that now you can use more messages than the first time and that you can schedule appointments with a few days of Advance. Ideally, before the appointment proposal, you have had a couple of WhatsApp / Telegram / Line conversations with her, and depending on her way of answering you, you will gauge how easy it will be to schedule a new appointment.

Let us see an example, this time I am not commenting on it so that you can identify each of the ingredients of attractive communication:

How to flatter her in an attractive way

One of the most basic rules of seduction is that you should never physically flatter a girl you want to pick up on because if you did, you would be acting as most typical frustrated guys. So, the "you are the prettiest girl I have ever seen" thing will never work for you. However, there is a way to flatter a woman attractively without looking like a "jerk," This is to pay her a compliment as if you were a couple.

This is a technique that you can use both in the game of seduction (when you are meeting a girl) and in the telephone game, where it will help you create a connection between the two. The examples that I present here are very good as always, but my favorite way of making a couple of compliments you have seen in the previous section is by sending a photo of the two in which you come out great.

Please send him a photo and tell him how handsome you are and what a good couple you make. You will create a very strong connection for two reasons, the first because you are giving a couple of compliments, and this is a very effective way to create a connection, and second Because with the photo, you are making her remember how she felt at the time the photo was taken, which surely was fucking awesome, and that is why you reinforce the connection. After this, she sure wants to see you again.

Let us see another case study:

(I send him a photo. Instead of saying that she is a sweetheart, I attractively compliment him saying that we are both sweethearts. The sweetheart is her, but thanks to this compliment from couples, I can create connection and awaken an emotion)

Ah, I saw them. They were the handosme pair in VIP   04:47 P. M.

(It works, the "hahaha" means that the compliment amused her, and I have awakened an emotion. Then, she reinforces the connection between the two, saying that we were the prettiest couple in the VIP area. And notice that it is she who uses the word "couple," more connection impossible)

Now that you know how powerful this technique is to create connection in the telephone game, what you must do is take advantage of it and every time you are having a great time with a girl, take photos with her and then use them in your WhatsApp conversations / Telegram / Line.

How to create an expectation

You have seen it in the examples throughout the book; one of the best ways to start the WhatsApp / Telegram / Line game, capture her attention, create curiosity, and make her invest in you is to use traps or baits. Thanks to these traps, you will get her to start asking you questions, and if you do it right, she may end up begging you to give her an answer or send her that photo you are talking about.

I am going to give you some examples:

How to be fun

Here, as in many other aspects, the most important thing will be not to screw it up. For example, do not text him with jokes that may be in bad taste, especially if you are still in the first phase of the telephone game and do not have much confidence.

Another important thing is that whenever you are going to make a joke about anything, first think about whether he is going to catch it, because then it is very bad that you must explain the grace to him on WhatsApp / Telegram / Line, and even if he ends up understanding it, it will be very difficult to get back into the rhythm of the interaction.

The best thing is that you do not worry too much about trying to be funny because just using the examples in this book will be enough to stir up an emotion in her and make her smile (and even laugh out loud). So, you should not feel pressured to make up great jokes and make her laugh; you already have everything you need.

Call to connect:

If you have already had your first date alone with her and everything went well, calling her will not be as risky as in the first phase. In any case, I only recommend that you do it if you feel like it and if she has asked you (many times it will happen to you that they will miss you calling them and saying, "let us see if you call me one day ...").

This call can help you make her want to see you more and get the next date more easily (if possible). I recommend that you make the call on the street, for example, when you are on your way to another site.

If you make the call from your home and without any noise or background sound, apart from the fact that it will be much easier for uncomfortable silences to appear when she asks or realizes you, what the subconscious will tell her is that you are a boring guy locked up at home with nothing to do.

However, if you make the call from the street while you hear traffic and people in the background, you can tell them that you are on your way anywhere because you are meeting some friends. In this way, your project that you are an interesting, busy man who goes out and interacts with many people. You can also take the opportunity to say goodbye to her at the best moment of the conversation (and thus make her want to see you again more) with the excuse that you have already met your friends.

Are You Enjoying This Book So Far?

Please take a few moments to write a review of the book. Reviews help spread the word out about your experience with the book so that others can make informed decisions. They also help me grow as an author.
Please leave a review for this book.

PART 4: You are dating her

Keep fun

Use spelling as humorous cues

T he "misunderstanding" strategy is a classic seduction that you can use both in person and the phone game. It consists in that you "misunderstand" something she says as if she were saying something provocative, flirting, or simply because it is good for you to make a joke. I repeat this concept since I will present you an example that loses meaning with the Spanish translation so that I will explain it to you:

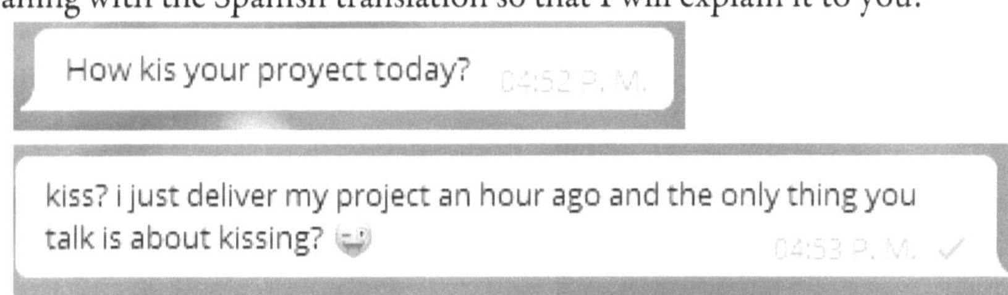

In this example, the misunderstanding comes from the American expression "make out," which, depending on the context, can mean to be successful or progress in something or kiss someone in a very sexual way. As you can see in the previous example, she used the first meaning of the expression, and the boy "misunderstood" it, using the second meaning to take the conversation to a more provocative terrain.

Now let us see an example of a misunderstanding that I used:

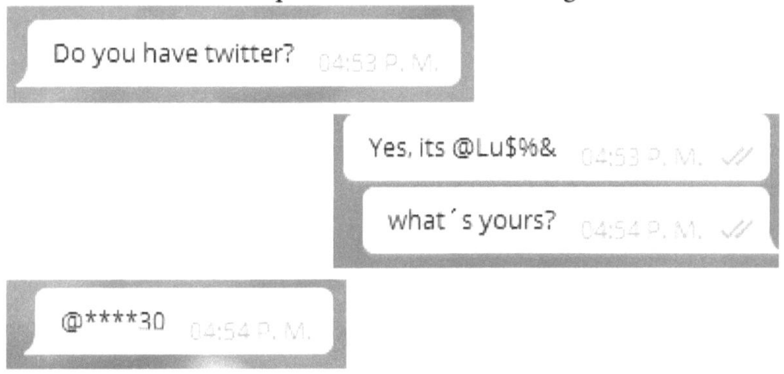

(Here comes the misunderstanding; I knew perfectly well that she was very young, and she was what she looked like, that is why I made the joke. Then she told me that she was 18 years old)

(It worked, she knew he was not serious and was amused by the "misunderstood")

Continuing with the sexual

ow to get started with sexual messages

Making sexual references or sexualizing your WhatsApp / Telegram / Line conversations can be very funny if she follows your game; you must keep some very basic rules in mind. You should only use this technique with girls you have already slept with, and everything went well; you should emphasize both (you and her), and you should make it "pop."

Moreover, how can you make it come up? The best way is to use "misunderstandings," as we saw in the previous section. Nevertheless, be attentive because she will often be the one who sends you easily "misunderstanding" messages so that you can steer the conversation towards the sexual arena.

You can also message yourself that she may misinterpret as having a sexual tone, and if she plays along, she wants to be sexting. On the other hand, if she does not play your game and is even offended, you can tell her that she was the one who misinterpreted the text because her eyes were dirty. There are many possibilities.

At this point in this example, there is a translation error in the example (some messages are repeated, and others are skipped), so I will copy it below. If your version of the book is already corrected, you should see something like this:

> It's a bit cold ... I had a coffee latte; it was made by divine power. Amazing!
>
> 05:03 P. M. ✓

> Hahahahaha! Omg! You mean you did it?!
>
> 05:04 P. M.

> Haha, no, it was a wizard... with a divine intervension.

> Ah... I want the filter profet do something magical too... Or maybe something magical to me ;P
>
> 05:13 P. M.

> Do you want to hang-out with the guy from Starbucks? Hes a little dummy TBH...
>
> 05:15 P. M. ✓

> Haha~ I love when you filter things yourself   05:17 P. M.

> Haha! I should have said "im going to taste out your p*ssy"
>
> 05:20 P. M. ✓

> Yeah.. That sounds hot 😳   05:21 P. M.

So, we will see a new example in which I made a very subtle sexual reference that worked very well to continue creating a connection between the two.

> Had you finished watch Misfits?   05:23 P. M.

(It is the girl from the previous example. She starts the conversation, and she does it regarding pop culture with which she knows that she will create a connection between the two; it is as if she is using techniques with me. Also, she initiates the conversation. Conversation with a question, which is an indicator of interest. The thing started well ...)

> I'm watching the third, but it's not the same ... do you know what my favorite moment of chapter one of the third season is?
>
> 05:24 P. M. ✓

(As always, I start by creating curiosity to get their attention, at this point, it would no longer be necessary, but it is always fun)

> Which one?

> when in the morning, the girl is going to ask the boy in bed if he wants me to make breakfast for her, and she is wearing a short shirt with nothing underneath

(I take advantage of his reference to pop culture that had nothing sexual to talk about a scene in which a couple spends the whole night fucking, and the next morning she gets up to prepare breakfast wearing only his shirt that covers her just enough. Something very similar to what happened between us a few days before, so I continue to create a connection between the two)

> Hahahahaha, I always wanted to do that

(It works; my answer amuses him, and he plays along. He says he has always wanted to do that because it is super typical of the movies that the girl appears the next day wearing only a shirt or shirt of the boy)

> The other day at my house I took you a shirt, but you didn't put it on!

(I forget about Misfits and talk about us, and I remind him that the other day when I took off his shirt to sleep in, he preferred to sleep naked. Obviously, at this point, the connection between the two is very high)

> Hahaha, is true

and you would have been great because it was one of those tight and short ... but better naked

05:28 P. M. ✓

Hahahahahaha but I'm more comfortable in that way   05:29 P. M.

(She feels comfortable talking about these things, and what is better, she is comfortable with the idea of sleeping naked to my side. I have successfully passed the conversation in sexting mode, and there is still a great connection between us).

PART 5: Appendix ...

143

Common questions and mistakes

ome questions

Do I have to respond every time a woman calls or texts me?

You are NOT obliged always to answer, and especially you will not be obliged when a girl has misbehaved with you. This is a good way to "punish" her and make her realize her mistake. If it takes you a long time to respond when you should not, she will be the one to change her attitude towards you and stop misbehaving.

Let us see a case study. I met Silvia and her friends at a cocktail bar, and just when I left, my friends

To spend some time alone with her, a song sounded, her friends came and took her to the dance floor, she did not think twice and left me with the word in her mouth. After a while, he wrote me the following ...

> I'm sorry, I didn't mean to turn my back on you, I'm not that rude
>
> 05:30 P. M.

> I'm sorry, I didn't mean to turn my back on you, I'm not that rude
>
> 05:30 P. M.

> I'm leaving, let's see us another day
>
> Have a good night 05:31 P. M.
>
> I'm out waiting for the cab 05:31 P. M.
>
> At least I wanted to say good bye properly 05:32 P. M.

(She was texting me for the rest of the night, and I did not reply to any of them because she misbehaved)

> Ok, another day you can appology :)

(I made it clear to him that he had acted badly but that he was not upset, smiley face at the end)

> Whenever you like, but let's go to a restaurant, is impossible to talk in a night club

(It works; she is the one who proposes to meet another day alone. This is another of those examples in which things end better than expected)

What about abbreviations?

Y ou probably have not heard anything, especially since the example is poorly translated, but do not worry. The idea is that in the United States, many abbreviations are used when chatting, such as LOL, OMG, LMAO, WTF, BTW, etc. However, we do not use them in Spanish, so you can safely skip this section.

Avoid common phone game mistakes

We are almost at the end of the book, and if you are a little anxious, you may have read it all in one sitting, now you are a little tired and do not give it the importance it deserves.

Read it as many times as necessary until you have assimilated it and have it burned into your memory because the errors it describes are made by practically 100% of the men who do not know the rules of the telephone game, and even many of those who if they know them, they fall like flies on these mistakes when they meet a girl they like.

You must read it and internalize it now, so when you meet a girl you especially like, you will not screw it up.

Nevertheless, I would like to add a couple more mistakes that I made (and I learned a lot) that I would like you not to make.

The first of them is to think that you have everything done, relax too much ... and suddenly not see a test coming and "eat it," that is, not overcome it. As you saw at the beginning of this book, women test us to make sure we are that attractive and confident man they deserve, and we call these tests.

Many men deceive themselves, and when they meet a girl they like, they go crazy and openly confess their feelings to her on WhatsApp / Telegram / Line ruining all their chances of having something with her. This is one of the worst things you can do, and it is possible that right now, you think that knowing it, you will never make this mistake ...

Well, I must warn you that you must be very careful because women love to test us, and if it is not born of you to confess your feelings, they will most likely try to make you do it will use the tests. So, you must always go with your eyes wide open for when this test is presented to you to overcome it; how? Never confess your feelings on WhatsApp / Telegram / Line.

Still not clear? Let us see the following case study:

We played the trivia game, you know, taking turns taking questions and pulling out dirty laundry. As you have already realized, playing this game, I was already making my first mistake, unnecessarily lengthening the WhatsApp / Telegram / Line conversation.

> Ok, I'm gonna make a direct question... What doyou want?
>
> 05:35 P. M.

(She throws me a test)

> you kidding? i want you!   05:36 P. M. ✓

(I responded by paraphrasing Kevin Spacey just before kissing Mena Suvari in American Beauty. She did not get the pop culture reference, and that is normal; when the movie was released, she was five years old... But that was not my big mistake)

> Your turn   05:36 P. M.

> What do YOU want?   05:36 P. M. ✓

> Now? Sleep. Tomorrow? Go to medic. To furure? Let's see later
>
> 05:37 P. M.

I was left with an asshole face looking at the screen of my iPhone, it was the second time this happened to me, and I could not believe it. Nevertheless, with this, I already learned, and luckily, I was able to solve it. However, on the previous occasion, when I did not pass the test, everything went to shit, so you must be very careful.

Remember, when they ask your questions to confess your feelings on WhatsApp / Telegram / Line, DO NOT DO IT!

The second error that I would like to add is that, as you practice with this book, you will see that some messages will work better than others, and of course, there is nothing wrong with reusing what works, right?

The only thing you should keep in mind is not to send the same message to two girls who are friends because, believe it or not, and they also send captures of their WhatsApp / Telegram / Line conversations when they flirt with boys.

I met two girls on Halloween, they were friends, and I gave each of them a card with my phone number because they did not have theirs to write them down. So, I wrote first to one of them and then to the other:

> Amber i hope you dont ask who i am after you read this?
> 05:39 P. M.

> Mmmmm, I'm sorry, who are you?
> 05:39 P. M.

> How many cool guys did you meet who gave you their card to point their phone number? Did you meet on Halloween?
> 05:41 P. M.

> Oh, look... The same you answered to my friend, what lack of creativity
> 05:42 P. M.

END. There was no way to redirect the interaction. A pointed error that I never made again.

PART 6: Appendix. Screenshots of a lifetime

We have left for the final part of the book a collection of screenshots taken directly from our mobile phones; in some of them, you will see how we successfully apply the techniques of our style. This is just a very small sample of what a life of Elite Seduction is for us, you will be able to see what we do and how we do it, but most importantly, you will be able to see what our attitude is what we achieve thanks to it.

Therefore, you have no excuse from this moment because you already know what you must do if you want to change your life ... you must start doing it.

My first success

On this occasion, I will tell you an anecdote that will be very personal; however, I would like to share it, there were many failures I had before reaching this point where now I am the one who writes on the subject, but you must never give up defeated in this and never throw a tantrum or think that all women or men are the same.

Consider that in many cases, you will not be successful in the First, but it is important to know what were mistakes you made during a conversation; if you are going to send a message that contains many lines, I recommend that you read it before pressing the send button, to be sure that what you wrote was Right.

I know that today there are options to erase the message and disappear it, and nobody knew anything. However, nevertheless if at that time it was online, it could reach to read what you wrote, and with so much anxiety and stress with which we live today, Seeing the message: "this text message has been deleted" can become badly thought by the person who receives it since sometimes we regret our texts and delete them, although in our case is not the same, good things may seem bad when we least imagine it.

I met this girl at a disco, she had come with some friends to go over a bridge, and during our conversation, my sense of seduction told me that the night could end very well for both of us ... However, before anything interesting could happen Between us, the ugly friend came very angry to tell her that this was a girls' night and blablabla, something very typical.

My sense was good, later at 7 in the morning, he wrote to me on WhatsApp / Telegram / Line to see us (you know why), although, by that time, it was too late. We were at my house David, Rubén, and I with three other girls.

Nevertheless, I liked the girl, and since she is not from around here, I am in the waiting rhythm right now. So I use a lot of my experience to be able to keep the conversation going, not only that if I do not draw their attention based on feelings and the most important thing always be as honest as possible in your questions, it is true that you should not reveal all the information no It is necessary, answer what you like, it is always better to say "I do not want to talk about that" or "I do not feel like talking about that topic," sincerity and security will always be a key point.

Keeping her warm

This is a girl that I met in a workshop (seduction during the day) that was being taught, that I kissed her on the mouth in the middle of the street 5 minutes after meeting her. After starting the conversation on WhatsApp / Telegram / Line as proposed, alluding to what happened between us, she reawakened those emotions, we generated many connections, and I began to excite her over the phone.

Deep down, it kept her excited because two weeks later, she would go to Barcelona again and what had to happen happened, that the bed was our best companion, and she was hoarse for a couple of days.

The Turkish Passion

Another girl I met at a party hooked up that same night, but I wanted to keep in touch.

I remembered that when we met, she was telling me that she loved to travel but that for various reasons she had not been able to travel as much as she would have liked and had some pending destinations such as Egypt, Turkey ...

I started the conversation by proposing a trip to connect by talking about travel, which interested her. It worked because I caught his attention, but he quickly gave me a test, making excuses that if I had no job and no money, I overcame it instead of going into logical mode and giving justifications of money, work, unemployment, and boring topics ...

The key was to bring him back to an emotional state using the trick of substituting words for signs "you and me = unforgettable journey." It worked like a charm, and we were able to spend a weekend with a very good offer that I found on a trip for two of the Turkish passion in a beautiful hotel in Istanbul.

Passing the test of rejection

The story with this girl was very interesting because I had to work hard. I met her with her friends one summer night, but back then, she had a boyfriend, and we just exchanged phones with the excuse that I am Public Relations and maybe I could pass them to a disco for free in the future. That night nothing happened.

A few months later we saw each other again, she no longer had a boyfriend, and after having a great time together for a long time I tried to kiss her ... but she made me a cobra. However, she continued to have a great time with me and me more, so I immediately understood that it was the test of rejection.

I kept trying, two, three, and even four cobras I took ... At the fourth time, she told me that she never kissed boys in discos, but her body language was telling me. Otherwise, she was more and more attached to me. Finally, on the fifth, we kissed, and everything changed. Look at what he wrote to me as soon as we parted.

Erotic stories

You must maintain consistency by the phone game after meeting her. This girl is friends with a good friend of mine and has had a partner for five years, but she saw me so sure of me and laughed so much with me one day when we ate with my friend that the emotions that I awoke in her seem to stop her thinking about her boyfriend every time she talks to me.

I have a very different style of communicating to that of the rest of the boys, and I always talk about an experience that we will live together, and she relives what I am saying, so, even if we have not lived this adventure, yet she already knows it. So, he was imagining, and apparently, he liked it. So, if the traffic light has a green light, take advantage of it, and keep pressing the accelerator.

Sexting with a horny

If you have Internet sex with a girl, it is called cybersex, and when you have it through WhatsApp / Telegram / Line, it is called sexting.

With this girl who did not live in the same city, we had been trying to meet for a long time, and one morning I used something that men believe can only be used in person, it is sexualizing (if you do not know this concept, we talk about it in Elite Seduction). It consists of talking about sex or what you would do to a woman through messages.

As you can see, she quickly enters the rag, she gets very horny, and we have a very hot time together. In the end, a couple of weeks later, he came to see me in my city, and we were able to finish what we had started on WhatsApp / Telegram / Line.

Doing things right from the start

If you have read Elite Seduction, you will remember that I mentioned this girl in the last paragraph on page 268 of the book. The 20-year-old Andalusian I met and had no high hopes of ever seeing again. Nevertheless, look where I had to do something right because she was the one who ended up writing to me to stay.

The point is that, if you start to get used to doing things well, do not be surprised that things start to happen to you that have never happened before, such as hot girls who write to you to stay (or even things many best ;).

You can see in the following screenshot how she started the conversation by writing a lot and showing much interest; from there, it was very easy to continue with the bolt sequence.

From now on, whenever they write to you like this, interpret it as if they are looking forward to seeing you.

Kiss Me

This is a girl I met in a bar, and we closed with the phone for closing on something. When she saw my social networks, she became interested in me because she saw that I hung out with many girls, and then my game began, and I started joking with her.

The problem that boys have on WhatsApp / Telegram / Line is that they speak in a very logical way and do not play tricks on the girls, and that is what I am going to teach you, which is what there is not. Because when you joke, sexualize or do sexting (sex by messages), it is much more fluid because of good vibes and closeness.

Messages from the trunk of memories

This girl was someone very special to me, and we already knew each other before. So, she wrote to see how I was doing and if I had any plans for that night. So, we went together to a disco where we had a great time, we held hands, we hugged, and when I left him at his house at dawn, a few minutes later I received this message.

WhatsApp / Telegram / Line is an excellent way to reconnect with girls you have not seen for a long time, but if you do not know how to use it correctly instead of a message like this, you may not receive any and have no idea where you screwed up. So, I will explain how to revive an old number with girls with whom you have not talked for a long time and had forgotten, but with whom you can playback by playing a good phone game.

In the "jacuzzi"

This was one of those nights that initially promised a lot and ended up being epic in the end. I was meeting at the disco with a girl I had already hooked up within the city, and she told me she was coming with a friend, so I called David del Bass to complete the team.

Nevertheless, I could not stay that night, in exchange he handed me the phone number of some of his friends who were also going to the disco. So solved, I thought, surely one of his friends would want to hook up with the friend ... Well, this was not what happened.

When we were all partying, my girl asked me, "Do you like my friend? Shall we have a threesome?". Of course, I said yes, but I had to think about how we were going to hook up ...

Total, I came up with a very crazy story that ended up working (I will tell you about it later because it has become our official routine to get threesomes), and almost without realizing it, the three of us ended up naked in the "jacuzzi" (bathtub) of my house. In the screenshot, you can see the following days, I continued talking about that with my girl by SMS, and we agreed that we would repeat it soon.

The curiosity of fucking a stranger

A very different girl that I met on the street and in her first message she told me that she had made her very horny because one of her dreams is that a stranger would make love to her in an office, that she had had that fantasy many times (but for I still did not keep conversations on WhatsApp / Telegram / Line on those dates, although it has stuck in my mind).

A girl who has tried to put me to the test many times while being horny. You can meet many very sexy girls on the street, but if you do not dare to sexualize on the phone or, more importantly, meet them on the street, these conversations will not arise on your mobile.

I have been able to sexualize adequately and to receive answers that did not happen to me before, nor by asking the genie in the lamp for wishes.

WhatsApp / Telegram / Line with a "dangerous" MILF,

I met this girl on a night out while teaching a seduction workshop with my students. There was much feeling from the first moment, and she was a 35-year-old MILF (horny mature) who was partying with her co-workers and taking her to fuck that night would have activated her whore factor.

I kept in touch by WhatsApp / Telegram / Line to have a second date and finish with it. As you can see, I use the hook "Well, I tell you one thing, and you will have to prove it" to keep her interested and thus get a date with her. He throws me a test about age, trying to see if that is a problem for me, but I managed to overcome it correctly by pretending it did not affect me and finally, we had a second date, and I spent the night at his house.

Tests and more tests

Life changes a lot when you understand the game of seduction, and you will already be realizing it. If what this girl told me that day on WhatsApp / Telegram / Line she told me six years earlier, she would have shifted vinegar.

With the time and place of the appointment already closed and without me asking her anything, she gave me a very long speech about how she was a difficult girl who did not hook up with just anyone and that all of us guys were shits for settling with the easy ones. Six years ago, I would have broken down thinking that I would have no chance with her, and I would have tried to convince her that I am different from other guys.

Nevertheless, now I watch the game and when she tells me all those things, what I understand is that she is qualifying, trying to show that she is a special girl (and she does it because she likes me) and that she is throwing me a test to see if she I respond as a typically frustrated uncle would.

If I had tried to convince him that I am not like all the other guys and that I am not going for the easy ones, I would have failed the test; how did I get over it? I told him that his theory seemed very interesting to me, but I had an even more interesting one, and I would tell him about it on our date ?.

We hook up.

Passing them

This is a girl I met working in a laboratory who came to undergo tests and ended up masturbating me in the bathroom of my research center. I can excite a girl a lot when I am in front of her but through messages.

Thanks to this book, I have discovered that begging and not answering instantly will arouse much interest from the other person because you challenge them. They are used to other people being always available, but they will notice you if you do not act like the rest.

It is so intense that it ended in a threesome

This conversation was very crazy, but I liked it because I managed it so well. She is the one who starts the conversation by telling me that she is very bitchy (that is, excited), but I frequently misinterpret her message by asking if she is excited or lazy (when someone says that she is very doggy, it can mean that she does not want to Do anything).

We had talked about having a threesome because I asked him, "what is the sexual fantasy that you most want to do?" and she told me to do a threesome. I told her that I had a friend who liked those things and finally it was she told me she wanted to do it.

We did, but I will tell you about that experience in another moment...

The great Lucian

I include this capture, even if it is not of a conversation with a girl, because that night was also epic, and because when I saw the WhatsApp / Telegram / Line, I broke down with laughter.

It turns out that I met Rubén at the party (a natural seducer who also appears in our book Elite Seduction); he asked me to finish the party at his house this time because he had to get up early the next day (we usually end up at mine). The problem is that I had a roommate, and there were only two beds.

The idea was to flirt very quickly and go home before his roommate so that he could sleep in the living room. So, we went out with very high energy, and in a while, we had already seduced two girls.

Since he had no battery left in his cell phone, he asked me to talk to his roommate and let him know that we were going there.

You can see what she wrote in the screenshot, but the important thing is that you can achieve what you propose with a good attitude; that day, we needed everything to happen quickly, and it did.

Playing with your emotions

A girl I met through a friend on social media. She knows what I do and said she would never say something nice to me because she did not want anything. They usually say that always from their logical reasoning, but when they see that they are having fun with you, they have fun, and that you make them feel different from the rest of the guys, they change their behavior.

If you want a girl to change her behavior, do not try to change her arguments; change her emotions.

I am your prince charming

I met this girl at the nightclub one night out. I invited them to a friend's house to continue the party, there were 3 of them, and we ended up having sex with them that same night.

I wanted to have a second date with her, and I wanted to apply the techniques with her with a girl you have slept with, trying to flatter her attractively, with an intimate theme, sex.

I gave her a compliment making her feel that for me, she is a special girl, and to encourage that the next time we see each other, sex is not something "bad," but a point of union between us and that it is easier for me to be able to get back have sex with her.

The girls using seduction techniques with me

I met this girl around the time I was working at the Serrano 41 nightclub on weekends. We used to see each other quite a bit and had already hooked up, but we only saw each other when we were partying.

That day he wrote to me to propose a date; he wanted us to meet out for the day the next time. Nevertheless, best of all, he used a seduction trick to create curiosity, leave me intrigued, and give me a better chance of closing the deal.

I was amused. I was with her... had to know what she wanted to ask me.

Playing tough to get me

This has been one of the most special girls for me in a long time, I met her on the street while eating a hamburger, and I felt an extreme obligation to stop her. It has been multiple stable relationships that I have had until she could not take it anymore and decided to sing me 40.

We can do two things: beg for forgiveness and change or try to change our emotions. I have never tried to change his thoughts; in fact, I let him continue, and I laughed with everything he put since I knew what he felt.

Two days later, we met again to commit our "misdeeds" ...

ATTENTION antipersonnel girls!

I wanted to share this capture because sometimes these situations happen, and if we manage them badly, we are out of the game.

I used a radar message that I have copied from Lucian because it works very well, and she responded with something that I did not expect. 100% logical message with emotional garbage.

These types of messages are like a minefield; in part, it is a test, and in part, she is telling you "the time is not right." The most common mistake he made before was to ANSWER THEM, trying to turn the situation around, and what he got was failing the test, entering a dialogue that did not contribute anything, and in the end, the girl disappeared.

Many men are tempted to respond to these types of messages, our protective instinct wants to come to light, but we have found that the best thing in these cases is NOT to respond, let a week or two pass and start from scratch applying the principles for girls that they do not respond or disappear.

On the first day

I think that in this capture, it is very clear how the game of seduction works.

This girl told me that she had gone shopping with a friend and that he had given her a great gift. She told me to make me jealous, and I told her.

Her answer clarifies many things, that friend is the typical frustrated guy who thinks he is going to hook up behaving like a "good boy" doing things like taking her shopping and giving her gifts ... but after two years of trying to hook up with her, he has not managed to NOTHING. However, I the first day, whoosh, why?

It was not for putting eyes on him, I assure you, it is all a matter of having a good attitude and knowing how to do things well, and thanks to that, we had a great time together.A waitress of 10

After making love to her, make her feel special. Otherwise, that girl will be dead to you because she will feel like one more.

This girl was a waitress at a disco, and she gave me her phone number. The next day I met her, and we ended up in a hotel doing everything imaginable. She had an extremely good time, but she felt like one more.

I saved her first message, which I thought was super sweet, and I sent it to her when she told me "that she was one more of all." Furthermore, that act told her that it was not one more for me and ended up sending me a photo of her in her underwear.

Women, if you make them feel special ... they will give you special things.

Sending me pictures of her ass

This is a girl I met on a website to meet people from your area. She told me she had a tattoo, and I told her that I could not get it out of my head and wanted to see it.

You can see how she sends me the photo with the tattoo on her lower back, but she also shows me her boobs and is in a thong. So clearly, you can see that she is very hot, and I took the opportunity she gave me to go further by asking her for a picture of her ass, and now, she sent me a picture of her ass on all fours passing my earrings.

So that not even an easy girl would feel bad, which is what happens to many after sending you photos when they get "buyer's remorse" I made an emotional connection talking about the destination, although she was still hot and eager to "Get on my tail."

She finally ended up getting on.

Fucking on the tiger

I met this girl one day when she was with her best friend making a bottle in the street; I greeted them and told them that we would meet inside at the disco. When I arrived, I told David del Bass that I had met two very hot girls outside... and so much that we were already making out within half an hour after they arrived.

After a few kisses, he asked me if we fucked, to which I answered yes, that we go home. Nevertheless, she told me it had to be right there because her boyfriend was coming to pick her up at any moment. So, there was no option; we ended up fucking in the bathroom of the disco.

A few weeks later, we met again, and this time, her boyfriend had gone on a trip for 15 days; you can see in the capture that he also came quite hot that night.

Self-confidence attracts women

This girl already showed interest in me because I made her so good in the day game. I could not have passed the test that he gave me, but I decided to make him feel emotions, and I used a seductive technique of substituting words for signs, which is very effective and would never have occurred to me.

Conclusion

Women are no longer the same, and they do not act as before, so you can no longer interact in the same way because you will not get anywhere if you want to seduce them, now you must have a stronger impact on their life, on their perception, you must change your way of proceeding.

You must get it into your head that if a woman answers you, it is not necessarily because she is interested in you, but it is most likely because you fill her self-esteem, she likes to know that there is always someone watching her, but that feeling does not pass from there, for what you are ultimately nothing more than a game that fills your ego.

You can notice that if you see that the conversation with her does not flow, that she answers you very little and after a long time, and that she does not advance in the intention of meeting you, she only limits herself to keeping her image before you.

Today's women are, for the most part, dependent egos; they seek attention on social networks, they want to swell their ego through the attention that men give them, but without any commitment and without considering the Their feelings, they only feel good when they realize that thanks to their beauty, they can have whomever they want at their feet.

DON'T BE ANOTHER SLUG IN THE STATISTICS

So, it is time for you to stand out, do not be just another statistic, do not be one more on their list, you must hit their ego, leave them in sight, focus on yourself, ignore them, treat them as if they were nothing, take time to respond to them and act. As if you were not interested. That attitude will cause an impact since they will not expect it, and thus they will be curious to know about you, someone different from all the rest who only idolize them and continue without doubting.

With the EXCESS of attention that women have in social networks, the most macho does not stand out; the ONE WHO CANNOT HAVE stands out. So, show her that YOU DO NOT CARE, and she WILL FEEL CHALLENGED to CARE.

DON'T CHASE HER, THEY DON'T LIKE IT. Do not be "another" who writes to increase their EGO.

Keep in mind that they can give you one of these three labels: "entertains me," "interests me," or "step of your face." It would help if you learned to differentiate well when each of these is.

Something that will make you attract her attention and stand out from the rest is that you are safe enough to call her, something that almost nobody does, and the rest of the time passes from her.

For example, you call her once a week, and then the rest of the week, you hardly speak to her on WhatsApp. This way, you connect better with her through your voice, and you awaken her interest in this contradictory attitude of spending the rest of the time with her.

Finally, the contradictory complement strategy is widely used by womanizers and extremely effective. It is about PASSING HER OLYMPICALLY, HAVING AN ATTITUDE THAT YOU LIKE IT LESS THAN A STICK, BUT 1 TIME OR 2 A MONTH YOU TELL SOMETHING VERY NICE OR LIKE YOU HAVE Much INTEREST, THAT YOU WANT TO SEE IT, and then you pass it on again.

All these strategies will help you arouse great interest in yourself and maintain it over time.

Did You Enjoy This Book So Far?

Please take a few moments to write a review of the book. Reviews help spread the word out about your experience with the book so that others can make informed decisions. They also help me grow as an author.

Please leave a review for this book.

Don't miss out!

Visit the website below and you can sign up to receive emails whenever Lucian Simon Ionesco publishes a new book. There's no charge and no obligation.

https://books2read.com/r/B-A-TLAP-PKPPB

BOOKS2READ

Connecting independent readers to independent writers.

Did you love *How To Flirt Through Social Media*? Then you should read *The Optimal Guide To Have A Perfect Date*[1] by Lucian Simon Ionesco!

[2]

I know that sometimes it is very *difficult* to say that things do not go the way you want to blame other circumstances. Nevertheless, perhaps many of the first dates you have had have not gone quite well because you do not know the correct way to go.

However, do not worry; here I am to guide you in all those doubts that may occur to you.

In this book, you will learn:

Ideas for optimal placesTips to have a good video callWhat to do on your first dateMistakes you should never make on your first dateThe second date theorySome personal experiences and more!

---

1. https://books2read.com/u/3R8rZR

2. https://books2read.com/u/3R8rZR

With this, I assure you that the first dates will be even better than the previous ones you have had to achieve a specific goal of what you are looking for.

When you are done reading this book, you will have gained a lifetime of experience in just a few short hours. The stories are interesting to follow, and the challenging concepts have been made easy to understand. So get ready to broaden your horizons and adjust your expectations because you are in for one hell of a ride!

Read more at https://www.facebook.com/pages/category/Publisher/Atelerix-Creative-Quill/.

About the Author

I'm 51-year-old; I have a degree in psychology, specializing in motivation and mental disorders.I'm a Brazilian Christian, and I define myself as straight, and I'm a vegetarian.

I grew up in an upper-class neighborhood. I was raised by my father and my mother, having left when I was young.

I'm currently single. My most recent romance was with an artist called Ophelia Dana Phillips, who was 12 years older than me. We broke up because Ophelia felt Lucian was too busy for the relationship.

My best friend is a chorus actor called Keira Morales. We get on well most of the time. I also hang around with Glenn Rees and Arran Davis. We enjoy worship together.

I have decided to start my work writing since currently, due to the pandemic, I require an additional income. With the support of the Atelerix publishing house, I want to start giving my general knowledge about everything I have studied in my city to swim all this time.

I hope that you fully recognize my writing and support me, especially if you have a loved one you can support with my knowledge; I will be more than happy to support me with a review of my book.

Read more at https://www.facebook.com/pages/category/Publisher/Atelerix-Creative-Quill/.

About the Publisher

The love and affection created the company we have for reading and writing. Atelerix creates and publishes written works based on the knowledge and unlimited imagination of people around the world.